THE LITTLE BOOK OF MIRIAM

THE LITTLE BOOK OF MIRIAM

JOHN MURRAY

To H. A. S. who won't read this book either, and to the memory of Katerina Clark, who introduced us

First published in Great Britain in 2025 by John Murray (Publishers)

6

Copyright © Miriam Margolyes 2025

The right of Miriam Margolyes to be identified as the Author of the Work has been asserted by her in accordance with the Copyright, Designs and Patents Act 1988.

All rights reserved. No part of this publication may be reproduced, stored in a retrieval system, or transmitted, in any form or by any means without the prior written permission of the publisher, nor be otherwise circulated in any form of binding or cover other than that in which it is published and without a similar condition being imposed on the subsequent purchaser.

A CIP catalogue record for this title is available from the British Library

Hardback ISBN 978 1 399 82661 7
ebook ISBN 978 1 399 82662 4

Designed by Nicky Barneby, BARNEBY *design & artdirection*
Typeset in 12/14.25pt Barbou by BARNEBY *design & artdirection*

Printed and bound in Great Britain by Clays Ltd, Elcograf S.p.A.

John Murray policy is to use papers that are natural, renewable and recyclable products and made from wood grown in sustainable forests. The logging and manufacturing processes are expected to conform to the environmental regulations of the country of origin.

Carmelite House
50 Victoria Embankment
London EC4Y 0DZ

www.johnmurraypress.co.uk

John Murray Press, part of Hodder & Stoughton Limited
An Hachette UK company

The authorised representative in the EEA is Hachette Ireland,
8 Castlecourt Centre, Dublin 15, D15 XTP3, Ireland (email: info@hbgi.ie)

'*Though she be but little, she is fierce.*'
Act 3, Scene 2, *A Midsummer Night's Dream*

(Well, you always have to have Shakespeare!)

CONTENTS

INTRODUCTION 1

A academia; accents; acting; adverts; afterlife; aging; agony aunt; air raid; amateur; America; animals; answering machine; antisemitism; AnuSol; apartheid; apostrophes; armchair acting; 'Arnie, Fuck you'; arsehole; art; 'As the Actress said to the Bishop'; audience; Australia. 7

B bacon; Bailey, David; balls; BBC; Beeb, saved by the; befriend, how to; belly; bike sheds; *Blackadder*; *Bleak House*; blood at the Crossroads; boring; bowels; breasts; Brexit; Broadmoor; bullies; burning your boats; Burton and Taylor; buttocks. 21

C Cadbury's Caramel Bunny; callipygian; Cameo; Camilla; *carpe diem*; cast your bread on the waters and it will come back sandwiches; centimorgan; charisma; cheesecake; children; Christianity; Christmas; cock-sucking; coffin; comedy; confidante; confidence; conversation; corpsing; costume drama; cracked on someone, being; crisps; cunt; cunt-face; curiosity. 35

D Daddy; dame, nothing like a; darlings, murder your; death; dentist; diamond; DiCaprio, Leonardo; dick; Dickens, Charles; die, always say; dieting; Dietrich, Marlene; direct, always be; direction; discipline; 'Do you like me?'; 'doctor in the house, is there a?'; documentarian; dogs; Dolly Fart-on; don't give up; dreams; dyke. **49**

E Edinburgh tattoo; Edward VII's weighing machine; Elephant Ethel; elephants; elocution; embonpoint; emotion; Escobar, Miriam; exercise; eyes. **63**

F face; Fagin; fail better; family trees; fandom; farting; fat; fellatio; Footlights; fortresses; free speech; friction; frightener; frocks; 'frummers'; fuck; 'Fucking hell! This is a fucking nightmare'; funeral. **75**

G gagging; Gamp, Sairey; gay; genealogy; gerunds; gin; gluttony; God; good advice; good girls; gossip; grave matters; groin-twitch; growing up; groynes; guests; Guides. **87**

H hairbrush; handbag; handjob; Harmony House; Havisham, Miss; heredity; herpes; holidays; Hollywood; home; horseradish; housework. **95**

I ice-breaking; ice cream; iced buns; identity; imposter; incontinence; Infanta of Castile; intelligence; internet; intimacy; intimacy counsellor; intuition; IRL (in real life); Israel. **107**

J jam; *James and the Giant Peach*; *Jane Eyre*; jealousy; Jesus; Jew, being a; Jewdar; John, Augustus; Johnson, Boris and Stanley; joke one; joke two. **117**

K kibbutz; kike; kindness; King, The; kissing; knickers; knitwear; koalas and kangaroos. **127**

L lady, being a; landlords; laugh; laughter; laziness; Leavis (and being a Leavisite); left-wing, becoming; lesbians; lift etiquette; 'like'; limelight, don't hog the; lines; living in a fridge; lodgers; London; look at me; love; lying. **135**

M make the most of it!; Manikin Cigars; manners; marches, going on; Margolyes; marmalade; marriage, the Ten Commandments of; maths; meanness; Meep; memory; men; Metropolitan Museum; migrants; Miriam; mobbed; moderation; money; moral compass; Mummy. **145**

N Napolitana, La; naughtiness; never forget; new friends; New Zealand; NHS; nipples; Northern Ireland; 'Norwegian Wood'; nose-picking; nudity. **161**

O OBE; 'Oh Miriam!'; old age (or the organ recital); *Oliver Twist*; Olivier, Laurence; one-off; onions; only child; openness; opera; oral fixations; orgasm; ostrich impression; out, coming; outrageous; outsider. **169**

P Pacific Palisades; Palestine; panda; parking; partner; Patriarchy; penis; period costumes; periods; PG Tips; pockets; politics; 'popular' culture; potatoes; Potter, Harry; pranks; probation; prompt; prunes and prisms. **183**

Q Quantocks; quarrel, never let the sun set on a; queen; queer; queuing; quiet, be; questionnaire; questions, asking; Quidditch; quoll ambassador; 'Quoth the Raven'. **201**

R rabbis; radio; radish; raising the fallen; rebellion; Reds (not in the Bed); regrets; relationship; restraint; retail violence; retire, don't; rider; roly-poly; rudery. **211**

S sanitary towels; Scorsese, Martin; secrets; semolina; sex; sherry; shit happens; shoes; shorts; *shtetl*s; small talk; Smith, Maggie; smoked salmon; social intercourse; soul; spam; speak out; Spice Girl; sports skills; stage fright; stickybeak; style; superstition; swear jar, a walking; swearing; Switzerland. **225**

T talented toddlers; *Tales of the Unexpected*; talk shows; tchatchkes; technology; teenager; tennis; tentacles; tents; Teresa, Mother; Thatcher, Margaret; *Today*; tone-deaf; too fat to go to bed with; Tories; trans; trans rights; transparency; Trojan horse; truthfulness; trust; *tsuris*; turnips. **239**

U umbrage; uncertainty; unconditional love; uncoupling; undergarments; understudy; unhappiness, unions; *University Challenge*. **255**

V vagina costume; *Vagina Monologues, The*; Vaughan, Frankie; Victoria; visions; *Vogue*, being in; voice-over; volatility; vulnerability; vulva. **263**

W   wardrobe mistresses; weapons; weight; whatever; whiskers; white lies; White Sniffs of Dover; 'wicked child'; Williams, Kenneth; winging it; woke; women are sublime; womyn; words; Workers Revolutionary Party; wrestling; wrinkles.   **273**

X   X-rated; xenophobia.   **283**

Y   YES; Yid, Gay; yoni; yourself, be; Youth is wasted on the young; Yumbo.   **289**

Z   zaftig; zest; Zionism; zodiac signs (pah!); Zoom; Zzz and so to bed.   **293**

AFTERWORD: Let Them Eat Cake   **299**

ACKNOWLEDGEMENTS   **302**

CREDITS   **303**

INDEX   **304**

INTRODUCTION

What do ARSEHOLES, APOSTROPHES and AGING all have in common? They're all entries for this informal and idiosyncratic dictionary of ME, Miriam Margolyes – an A–Z collection of wit and wisdom, insights, jokes, stories and aphorisms that I hope will touch your heart, kickstart your brain, and leave you in stitches. (Well, that's the cover sorted, then!)

Let me introduce myself:

> Actress, agony aunt and voice of AnuSol; BA Cantab, Blue Badge holder and BAFTA winner; Cadbury's Caramel Bunny, Documentarian, nothing like a Dame, Miriam Escobar, Farter by appointment, Geriatric, Infanta of Castile, Jew, landlady, Mother of the Company, Not remotely bi, OBE, quoll ambassador, Professor Sprout, Troublemaker, University Challenger, *Vogue* cover girl, Lady Whiteadder, sometimes X-rated, Gay Yid, Zoomist – and very pleased to see you again.

Welcome to my *Little Book of Miriam*. It's a little bit of me, a little bit of what you fancy, a little bit naughty, and, not entirely like me, it's small but perfectly formed. Forget coffee table books – this one has rather been cunningly constructed with your smallest room in mind. As you'll see when you get to my entry on BOWEL MOVEMENTS, from my earliest years I have been taught to appreciate the importance of regular visits and then to discuss them unrelentingly at the breakfast table. Lavatory visits should be about entertainment *and* relief and I hope to provide both herein. (Herein not Heroin!) Furthermore, in deference to your ever-decreasing attention span, I've kept it short, sweet and alphabetical.

Perhaps you're wondering why I've written another book. Well, for the money obviously (as always) but it's more than that. In these pages I'm offering my memories, thoughts and anecdotes of a sweeter, more humane world. Full disclosure: be prepared for some smut and swearing.

The funny thing about being eighty-four (Jesus Christ, EIGHTY-FOUR!) is that when you look back through your life, a surprising logic comes into focus. It makes me realise that I have been an outspoken old lady ever since I was a little girl – all my life whenever I have seen injustice, whether it's a bullying teacher, apartheid or Israel's treatment of the Palestinians, I have felt compelled to speak out.

I may exude confidence but being an actress makes you good at pretending everything is OK – especially when it really isn't. Every acting job, every audition, puts you up for rejection. It goes with the territory and believe me, it's a recipe for paranoia, the drinking of gin and the eating of far too many choccy biscuits ... What makes me most anxious, however, is the fear of disappointing you, letting you down, being boring, unhelpful, or worst of all, bland.

We all have our key stories, of course, and you might well recognise some of my favourites from various therapy sessions on The Blessed Graham Norton's sofa. But while I have no wish to harangue, I do have a serious purpose. I believe in fairness and fun, free love and free speech. And all of them are under threat. We desperately need an antidote to naysayers, belittlers, Nigel Farage and everyone who says 'whatever.' And I'm hoping that this little book might do the trick.

What a fucking awful world we live in! There's no denying since I last spoke to you that everything has turned upside down. Truth has become alternative, refugees have become criminals, Criminals have become Presidents and all we do is scroll through our phones. Not good enough. The bad guys seem to be winning everywhere but I'm not giving up …

Why are you either obsessively doomscrolling, surfing through disasters into depression, or ostrich-like, burying your head in the sands of sudoku, the cooking pages or property porn, while the cunts in power make yet more money and hang on to it? We've all been stunned into passivity but it's never too late for a wake-up call.

One day in 1969, I came back from rehearsals to find my kitchen ceiling had fallen down. (Bear with me: there is a purpose to this story even though I never got to the bottom of what caused it.) Heather was working in Kuala Lumpur at the time and I wrote and told her all about it. When, eight months later, she came back to London, I met her at Paddington. As we walked in through the front door together chatting away,

I blithely flung my handbag onto the pyramid of plaster and concrete that was still taking up half the room.

Heather was appalled: 'Haven't you fixed that yet?' Somewhat sheepishly, I had to admit I'd long since stopped even noticing it. The rubble had become part of the furniture. That was my way of dealing with catastrophe, to pretend it wasn't there. And that's exactly the behaviour we're all guilty of now.

Catastrophe is staring us in the face and we're ignoring it; AI and the return of the Far Right threaten our future and the lunatics have taken over the asylum. Those big swinging dicks around us need to be circumscribed. We have a fight on our hands, folks and what we both mustn't forget is that there is YOU and there is ME and together we are part of the army against that stupidity. It's time to join the resistance and make a stand – so let's find the Truth and have a laugh while we're looking for it. Here's to Making America Small Again! (And while we're at it, Russia too.)

4

We used to look into people's eyes and not at screens. And we can again.

People are always asking me for advice but now I really think about it, my rules for a good life boil down to just three things:

> BE OPEN: My secret is that I have no secrets – and never have had.
>
> BE KIND: I'm very keen on being kind. Put love in your sandwich, not shit.
>
> BE BRAVE: these are indeed scary times. People are burning books. (Please look after this one.)

Because ... the moment is now. This is not a dress rehearsal. It's time to Carpe that Diem. And Save Our Souls.

Everyone needs a hug – and I hope that my little book might offer the arms around that you need.

ACADEMIA: Mummy had an exaggerated respect for Academe. She left school at fourteen and her university was 'Retail' – she served in her sister's dress shop in Peckham Rye. Her dream was for me to go to Oxford and marry a doctor. While I didn't do either, I've inherited her veneration for learning. Perhaps that's why I once said I would never fuck anyone without a PhD. Haven't stuck to that one, admittedly.

ACCENTS: The English are a snobby lot and coming from the landscape we're born into and the voices we hear as we grow up, our accents reveal us; categorisation and judgement follow. Used as clues to a person's background, they enable and reinforce social exclusivity. I'm lucky. I can change my voice. I've made money and friends using different voices – never to defraud, only to reach people. It's all down to Mummy, who was determined I would not inherit either her lower-class, South-East London Jewish voice nor Daddy's native Glasgow sounds. I was packed off to school elocution lessons and thus acquired a sharp ear: I could hear the difference, and that sharpened my awareness of class separation. But it comes at a price. Imagine sounding like Jacob Rees-Mogg all your life. Now whenever I want to approach a stranger, whether to ask the time or to use their loo, I often use the Scottish accent inherited from my father, rather than my own, upper-middle-class vowels. Scottish has a pleasant and trustworthy sound, and it relaxes people.

ACTING: I entered a precarious profession where a short, fat, Jewish girl with no neck dared to think she could stand on a stage and be successful ... I may have a talent for acting, but truthfully,

I am incapable of doing anything else. Actresses were once thought of as whores, some have ended that way. The orifice of choice was always the mouth.

ADVERTS: The first adverts I became aware of were in *Daltons Weekly*. 'NO BLACKS, NO IRISH, NO CHILDREN'. But thankfully, that wickedness has gone. Much later on, I learned from a beloved colleague, Marise Hepworth, that I could supplement my BBC Drama Repertory Company income by doing voice-overs for radio and TV commercials. I have sold many strange things in my time, everything from anal suppositories to chocolate, tea bags to sanitary protection, insurance to cigars. They bought me at least one house. I've interleaved a few of the more amusing ones into this book.

AFTERLIFE: I don't believe in God and terrible things are done in the name of religion. Wars are fought, people are killed, lives are diminished by religion ... but I admit there must be something that I don't know, because I don't know everything – nobody can, or does. But the afterlife had better come while I'm alive – I can't waste time waiting for it. My old therapist, Margaret Branch, used to say that 'it might be a party ... I think it's going to be a party.' Let's hope so.

AGING: is not a choice: you either die or you age. It is the attitude that defines the experience. We learn from watching our parents. My father lived to be ninety-six and aged very well: but my mother betrayed her body by over-eating and it took its revenge. After two devastating strokes which paralysed her and took away her speech for the last seven years of her life, she died at sixty-nine. Not to be able to speak is now the thing that most terrifies me. But you can't spend your last years in terror. You mustn't shut yourself away from the world. I'm not some giddy idiot tottering off into the future with two sticks and an insane smile: of course I am miserable, just not all the time. Don't be lonely. Be brave, join the University of the Third Age, or a lunch club. And start pelvic floor exercises NOW.

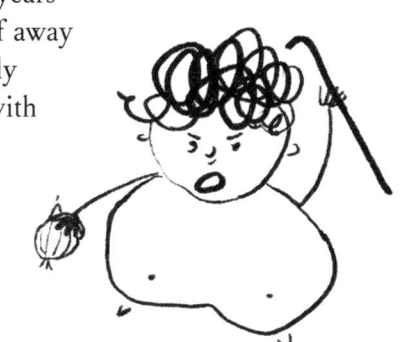

AGONY AUNT: The agony aunt I most admired and deeply miss was Claire Rayner. She spoke fast and truthfully. I don't mess about either, but when *This Morning* set me up as an agony aunt, I don't think even they expected my bluntly telling one viewer that she should leave her husband (he sounded such a pig), another that she should go on a diet, and a third to try talking to her aggressively horrible neighbour 'And if that doesn't work … just throw shit over the wall.' Never be afraid to bring smegma into a conversation – it can help!

AIR RAID: I was conceived in an air raid. Daddy was forty-two, Mummy thirty-seven; they were relatively old to be having a first child. But it was deliberate: most newly married couples try to have children, but for ten years my parents had tried not to. Two of Mummy's cousins had died in childbirth, and she was terribly afraid that the same fate would befall her. But, at the beginning of the Blitz, the terror of an air raid pounding above the cellar where they were sheltering finally allowed Daddy in – and me to be born. Mummy always said that was why I had curly hair.

A

AMATEUR: I had a falling out with Glenda Jackson once. I cannot remember what it was about but I called her a cow, and she called me an amateur. I think she won that one! But having since had the joy of judging the best Amateur Drama Society in the UK, thanks to Sky TV, I don't share her scorn. We could all learn from the passion of those untrained actors.

AMERICA: I'm not seduced by America, especially now since the Orange Turd has been voted in for a second time. I share Dickens's view. This is from a letter he wrote to his friend William Macready in 1842:

> This is not the republic I came to see. This is not the republic of my imagination... And England, even England, bad and faulty as the old land is, and miserable as millions of her people are, rises in the comparison... Freedom of opinion! Where is it? I see a press more mean and paltry and silly and disgraceful than any country ever knew – if that be its standard, here it is.

ANIMALS: Never act with children or animals, they say. I have pungent views on the first and much prefer the latter. I have voiced many kinds of animal in my time; I've been a snake, an owl and a glow-worm, but my favourite of all was the mother dog, Fly, in *Babe*.

Fly was practical, affectionate and shrewd, based on my childhood pet, a Scottish Border collie called Whisky. It was Fly who taught Babe not to be a doormat; if you let people doubt you, even just for a second, they'll trample all over you ... of course, she was talking quite literally about sheep, but I still see the truth in it as an invaluable life lesson. In the scene, the harder poor Babe tries to herd the sheep like a dog, the more the sheep jeer until, as Fly, I teach him that he has to dominate them – 'Do that and they'll do anything you want ... We are their masters, Babe. Don't let them doubt it!' The film company made me record Fly twice, as my original Scottish accent flummoxed the Universals. Never mind, I got two fees, two First Class trips to Australia, and I made friends with Chris Noonan, a great director. Win win – woof woof!

ANSWERING MACHINE: This is a true crime story but I've changed identifying details to avoid legal action. For me, answering machines have always doubled as quiet secretaries and as an auditory archive. Thus, in the early days, my outgoing messages were long and detailed, giving a full account of my daily activities plus comments on events. In 1978 I was appearing in a great play, let's call it *Cloud Ten* by Winston Churchill. Rehearsals were made complicated by an ongoing row with one of the actors.

I recorded as follows. 'Today is Tuesday, October 5th. 1978. I am shopping in the morning probably at Sainsbury's, then doing a voice-over at John Wood studios for a vaginal cream and later taking the tube to the Royal Court Theatre for a performance of *Cloud Ten*, where I have the misfortune to be working alongside HC, one of the most unpleasant and unstable people I have ever met. Please leave your message after the beep.' Unfortunately, one of my callers couldn't resist telling the identified actor about this message and they rang in to listen for themselves. The following message was left on my machine. 'This is HC speaking. I have listened to the defamatory message about me on this machine and so has my lawyer. Unless you publish an immediate retraction on this machine, we will press for damages in the Courts.' I phoned *my* lawyer who confirmed that I had indeed been defamatory and must issue a retraction as requested.

    The next day I did so. 'Today is Wednesday, October 6th. I will be shopping in the morning probably at Sainsbury's, then doing a voice-over at John Wood studios for a small cigar and later will be taking the tube to the Royal Court Theatre. I unreservedly retract my remarks left on this machine yesterday about my fellow-actor in the wonderful play there, *Cloud Ten*, whom I quite wrongly described as being one of the most unpleasant and unstable people I have ever met. Please leave your message after the beep.' When I got home after the show that night, approximately seventy people had phoned in to hear my message and left messages, many laughing hysterically, some even agreeing. A certain *froideur* remained after that incident between myself and the actor in question. Honestly, you can't be too careful with machines.

ANTISEMITISM: Nobody likes Jews, but today antisemitism has an excuse to flourish as a result of the appalling Israeli policy towards the Palestinians. I don't feel an allegiance to Israel, but what happens there concerns me. Antisemites have now found a justification for their vile bigotry. But to hate and attack Jews because of your feelings about Palestine is *wrong*. It's the Israeli government's persecution of Palestinians that's evil – not being Jewish. It's possible to be proudly Jewish and vehemently anti-Zionist. I am.

ANUSOL: Time for another insertion ... AnuSol clearly understood my deep recognition of the sanctity of a good bowel movement. I have been the nonjudgemental voice of their cream for years now:

> [*Picture images of curvaceous fruit and veg – a red apple, a peach, pear, tomato, a butternut squash, a beetroot, and finally a majestic aubergine, passing across the screen.*]
> BUMS. We don't tend to talk about them but one in two of them may get piles. Itchy, sore pains in the posterior [*This bit accompanied by images of a lemon beside a grater, or a prickly buttock-shaped cactus*]. Sound familiar? Use AnuSol, the UK's number one piles treatment. Developed by experts to soothe itching, relieve discomfort, and calm inflammation. For fast, long-lasting relief from piles, trust AnuSol.

APARTHEID: The injustices white South Africans imposed on their Black countrymen was what first ignited my political activism when I was at Cambridge. Even my right-wing parents agreed. Our cousins from South Africa had stayed with my grandparents before Mummy got married. She remembered the way they threw their clothes on the floor, expecting a servant to pick them up.

I have always felt an outsider – as did my parents. The unfairness of the apartheid regime enraged me, and that's why I volunteered to work in the campaign office of the Anti-Apartheid Movement in London and demonstrated outside South Africa House many times. Years later, after Nelson Mandela's release, Antony Sher and I were invited to a function at the same building; it was strange to be walking as a guest into the place that had been a symbol of everything I hated. But it showed that things can improve. Now I'm not so sure.

APOSTROPHES: My mantra explaining when to use this misused and misunderstood punctuation mark is: 'An apostrophe is a tombstone for a dead letter.' It works because of the power of the word 'tombstone'. As you say it, you see the tombstone rear up into the shape of an apostrophe. Now say after me …

ARMCHAIR ACTING: I was in a production of *The Widowing of Mrs Holroyd* by D. H. Lawrence. Mr Holroyd, a miner, is fed up with his wife. One night, he goes to the pub and brings two tarts home with him to teach her a lesson. I was playing one of the tarts and my direction was to sit down on a chair and act sozzled. However, in the period between the dress rehearsal and the first performance a few hours later, the chippies – the carpenters of the theatre – had attached castors to the bottoms of the legs of the armchair in which I was to sit. But no one had told me. So, when I plonked myself heavily in the chair, as if totally plastered, it felt as if it was moving down the raked, heavily sloping stage. I assumed it was the power of my acting, that I had so perfectly embodied the drunken tart, I was imagining my rolling progress – but no! I really was moving! The chair (and I) slid slowly but inexorably down to the edge of the stage. Then it rolled off, tipping me on top of an unfortunate punter in the front row. Amazingly, I wasn't hurt – the punter, luckily, also largely survived – but neither of us could speak, we were laughing so much. Eventually, I somehow managed to get back on stage, someone hoicked the chair up as well, and the show went on.

'ARNIE, FUCK YOU': I have only worked once with well-known bodybuilder and politician, Arnold Schwarzenegger. *End of Days* was a sublimely silly film, destined never to trouble even the longest of Oscar longlists. Arnie was an ex-cop on a mission to stop Satan conceiving the Antichrist in the final hour of the millennium (well, it was filmed in 1999 at the height of pre-millennial panic) and I was playing the Devil's servant Mabel. In the anxiety of our uncomfortably physical rehearsals, I once allowed a medium-strength fart to escape. Arnie leapt upon my transgression. How dare I? How disgusting it was. He couldn't let it lie, constantly bringing it up, in extreme tones of shock and revulsion. A few days later, we were filming our final fight. I failed to kill him, first with a grandfather clock and then with a grand piano. Lying on the floor, my throat sliced in half by a glass table, Arnie had me pinned down, utterly at his mercy. It was then he delivered the *coup de grâce* (or should I say, *coup de disgrace?*). He farted, loudly, purposefully and malevolently, directly into my face – and then laughed uproariously. He did it deliberately because he knew he was the star and could get away with it – and that I couldn't get away. My death throes in a miasmic cloud of Schwarzenegger sulphur were informed by real suffering. I was really cross and shouted, 'Fuck you, Arnie!' He clearly felt that he'd had the last laugh but it was too good a story to keep to myself and now, hopefully, the last laugh is *yours*.

A

ARSEHOLE: This insult really makes me happy. I enjoy its visual specificity. In my mind's eye, the small, puckered circle that is unmistakeably the anal opening is superimposed on the face of the offender, and my rage is reduced by the resultant image. You can't hate an arsehole; you can laugh at it, then feel faintly disgusted, and the fury is assuaged.

ART: I love Art but can't do it (rather like ice-skating). At school Miss Hardy consistently ranked me bottom in every Art exam, which was just but painful. Patrick Bade's Lockdown Lectures on Zoom have re-energised my passion and inspired me to design my own T-shirt (a self-portrait, naturally).

'AS THE ACTRESS SAID TO THE BISHOP': Conveying a medley of sexual games and mutually pleasing activities crossing all class boundaries, this phrase was initiated by the late, great Beryl Reid. She also offered 'As the Art Mistress said to the Gardener', which never fails to raise a smile and a suspicion of naughtiness. Apparently, the French have their own version: '*Comme disait le* *hérisson en descendant d'une brosse à chaussure*' ('As the hedgehog said when getting off a shoe brush'). Don't ask!

AUDIENCE: Give me an audience and I'm young again. Audiences revive and delight this old Thespian. Scared beforehand of course, but once I leave the wings, I fly.

AUSTRALIA: I became an Australian citizen in 2013 but it was falling in love with Heather in 1968 which made me an Aussie. After fifty years, the insertion became a fiscal reality. The Continent (as opposed to me – the Incontinent) is a wonderful place, but the less it aligns itself to America, the more its greatness will shine. I've come up with a little Aussie A to Z:

> A is Australia, ABC and the Alice (Springs);
> B is for Broken Hill, Bondi beach, budgie smugglers
>   and let's hear it for Bogans;
> C is for the Clarks (Manning and Katerina) my
>   first Australian family – but also for Chlamydia
>   (it's killing the koalas) and Chunder
>   (Aussie vomit);
> D and E are both for Dame Edna, waving gladioli
>   from the Great Beyond;
> F is for First Nation – this country was theirs first;
> G is Gough (Whitlam) sacked by QE2 for doing his
>   job and the other Good Australians;
> H is for Heather, the love of my life and Hawke, Bob –
>   today's puny politicians need to raise their game;
> I adore being an Australian;

J is for Julia Gillard (she made me a citizen) and Clive James;
K is for Kangaroos and 'Kin Hell;
L is for the Larrikin spirit;
M is for Magical Melbourne;
N is for 'No Worries!'
O is for Outback and for an Ovation (standing of course) at the Opera House;
P is for Possums and Pavlova;
Q is for Qantas;
R is for Robertson (my home) and Gina Rinehart (my least favourite Australian);
S is for Sydney;
T is for Tim Tams – my ultimate destruction;
U is for Uluru the sacred rock;
V is for Vegemite;
W is for Wallabies;
X is for Four X;
Y is for Yoni (it's where I learnt to steam it);
Z is for zonked.

Over and Out and G'Day.

BACON: I have never eaten bacon, and can't bear the smell although I am told I would love it. I will live and die a Jew, with my culture intact but minus the religion that is at the heart of it.

BAILEY, DAVID: I met David Bailey at the first-night party for *The Threepenny Opera* in 1972. There was a louche lesbian flavour to this affair, hosted as it was by a titled lady who was Hermione Baddeley's squeeze. The elegant all-white Syrie Maugham room, so bright and bleached that it was blinding, was filled with beautiful people – and me. I made a beeline for the only other person who didn't fit in. David was by far the un-poshest person there. Already a well-known photographer, he remained resolutely unimpressed by the preening around him. We had a funny conversation, perhaps because I was the only person in the room, male or female, who didn't fancy him – or indeed recognise him. When I asked, 'What do you do?' he laughed and said, 'I like birds.' I thought he meant of the feathered variety and so started talking to him, assuming he was a twitcher. When I meet someone, the first thing I try to do is to find common ground. He became more amused. I asked his name and when he told me I was overawed; of course, I knew who David Bailey was. We ended up swapping numbers and he said, 'You're an interesting bird. Come to my studio, I'll photograph you.' I always wished I had … until I read his autobiography and learned there that he only loved women who were thin and had small breasts – 'I don't like big udders.' Goodness knows what he would have made of mine!

But never say never! I've just looked him up and to my amazement, he's still alive. TO BE CONTINUED!

BALLS: I like balls. I enjoy their symmetry. If the balls were there without the cock, I'd be laughing.

BBC: These three initials are engraved on my heart. No other entity, apart from Newnham College, Cambridge, has had such a beneficial, indeed thrilling effect on my life. The founder of the BBC, the very tall Aberdonian Lord Reith, described the aims of public service broadcasting as Information, Education and Entertainment. These should remain, in my opinion, the three pillars of the BBC today. Successive governments try to hobble it by insisting on a fake 'neutrality' that requires an abdication of moral & intellectual responsibility. Jeremy Paxman & Stephen Sackur would have rejected these gutless panel discussions when every point of view is given the same attention. The Corporation's feeble current state reflects our fear of moral clarity but the BBC is vital to us all and *must* survive.

BEEB, SAVED BY THE: After leaving Cambridge and two frustrating years of selling encyclopaedias and probing passers-by about their contraception strategies, I finally got an audition. I arrived at Broadcasting House in Portland Place, London W1A 1AA, and announced to Norman Wright and John Bridges: 'I am now going to give you an example of my astonishing versatility.' No hiding my light under a bushel! I had decided on an improvised railway journey in which I played all the characters in the compartment. I hadn't scripted it; I'd just made a list of the accents that I wanted to show them, and then had a conversation between all the characters, making it up as I went along. A week later, a letter arrived: 'You did a very good audition and we are sure that we are going to be able to offer you some work in the future.' Years later, they told me that it was the most astonishing audition they'd ever heard because I switched between so many voices – male, female, Scottish, Yorkshire, Brummie, Cockney, all the regions, all the ages, French, German, Aussie, etc. I had been saved by the Beeb. In such a situation, Modesty is pointless.

BEFRIEND, HOW TO: I'm good at making friends because I need them. I love meeting new people; and when I talk to them and laugh with them, I feel like a flower opening in the sun. I am always direct. I say to them, 'I want you in my life. Don't go away. If you don't want that, you'd better say so now, otherwise it's going to get embarrassing.' And luckily, so far no one has ever said, 'Miriam, stop right there. NO, I don't want to be in your life.'

BELLY: I inherited my belly from my mother. I remember noticing that her belly hung down and flopped about. And I thought, 'Oh that's awful. I'll make sure I never get to look like that.' Well, it's happened. I can't blame childbirth, as Mummy did. My belly was made all by myself, through years of over-eating and under-exercising. Now it's my overhanging nightmare – and I have to put up with it.

BIKE SHEDS: Sex education at school, or at home, was non-existent. It was in the bike sheds that we learned about sex – the only information I was ever given was by people of my own age. It was the County Scholarship girls with their lipstick and petticoats and bold gazes who were the prime source of all sexual knowledge. There was a class divide between them and us City girls (who were the swots); consequently, we knew all about the periodic table but nothing about anything below the waist. Once we got to fourteen and fifteen, *everybody* was comparing notes in the bike sheds. But we swots had no data to speak of. Luckily for us, red-haired Carol Reay (who's now dead, alas) was the star of the bike sheds, the authority on sexual intercourse, and equally generous in sharing her hands-on experience. Carol was lustful and enjoyed sex and wanted to help us enjoy doing it too. We were communing with a teenage Wife of Bath. She proudly described the joys of youthful cunt completely without smut and subterfuge. Alas, vaginal prowess wasn't an A Level subject at Oxford High School – if it had been in the syllabus she would have been Head Girl. We hung on her every pronouncement. 'Always take some Vaseline with you,' she advised. We were baffled but immensely curious. I still carry Vaseline with me everywhere – but today I only use it as lip salve.

BLACKADDER: I like to think of myself as a proper actress (never actor) but I accept that I am more recognised as an 'over-actress'. Take the TV series *Blackadder*, in which I appeared three times – as the libidinous Infanta of Castile, then as the deranged Puritan Lady Whiteadder, and finally as Queen Victoria, coupled with Jim Broadbent as my Prince Albert. Mandie Fletcher, the first woman director in TV comedy I'd come across, was key to *Blackadder*'s success. I've never met her since those days and I wish to thank her now for her brilliant handling of those wilful boys and of me, scared stiff of not being funny or matching the combined talents of a willowy Tim McInnerny, a rubber-faced

Rowan Atkinson, Tony Robinson, and the twin gods, Fry and Laurie. These boys didn't mind my being funny, they relished my generosity with my breasts, and my heavy-handed bashes with **TURNIPS**. They weren't afraid or disgusted. And have remained my friends to this day.

BLEAK HOUSE: I still get overexcited at the first chapter of *Bleak House*, surely one of the best openings of any novel:

> LONDON. Michaelmas Term lately over, and the Lord Chancellor sitting in Lincoln's Inn Hall. Implacable November weather. As much mud in the streets, as if the waters had but newly retired from the face of the earth, and it would not be wonderful to meet a Megalosaurus, forty feet long or so, waddling like an elephantine lizard up Holborn Hill.

And you're there! Pulled into the story – no escape. I weep and I laugh and it grips me. The best literature has that effect on you. I want everyone to go back to the great books and enjoy them. These little slices of literature have stayed with me since my schooldays; they continue to stimulate my brain and I munch over them, like delicious leftovers. They are for everyone, not just for the educated classes. Dickens was the first great artist to be appreciated by *all* classes, probably until Elvis came along!

BLOOD AT THE CROSSROADS: Early in my career, I got the chance to audition for *Crossroads*, a now defunct soap opera set in a motel in the Midlands, which used to go out on ITV several times a week and was very popular. It was hardly distinguished television but it was a solid job, and I needed one.

I took the train up to Birmingham for the audition and arrived at Pebble Mill Studios. I was just about to sit down when I felt that ominous trickle. My period had started and I was unprepared. I rushed to the nearest loo. Fifty years ago, there was a big brown vending machine containing Southalls Sanitary Towels in every lady's lavatory. I had my money ready, I put it in the slot, yanked open the drawer– and it snapped back with my finger still in it. I was trapped! I was pulling and pulling in agony. Finally, the drawer snapped open and released my lacerated finger, pouring with blood. I held it under the cold tap for a minute, quickly fixed myself up in the loo, and rushed back to the audition where they were irritatedly waiting for me.

I was just about to begin the reading when I noticed my script was covered in blood, the pages sopping and seeping with it. I looked at my audition committee sitting at the desk. Normally stony-faced, their mouths were hanging open and they looked green. I said, 'Oh I'm terribly sorry. You see, my period's started ......'

As the word 'period' left my mouth, I could see their faces wobble and contort with horror; they now looked as if they might throw up. I hastened to explain: 'No, no, it's not ... umm ... IT'S MY FINGER!' and I quickly gathered my wits and launched into the audition piece for a supposedly conventional Birmingham housewife who always wore a headscarf – my Brum accent was spot on. Period or no period, I got the part.

BORING: Some people just are, even good friends. Actually, especially good friends. And if this friend is going on and on, well, say so. I believe in the direct approach: 'Did you know you're being a bit boring?' If they bristle, just say, 'Oh come on, it doesn't mean you *are* boring, it just means you're *being* boring.' Then you give them a hug. Actually, that was quite boring.

BOWELS: Before I left home for school every day, my doctor father expected a detailed report on the appearance, consistency and frequency of my bowel movements. I ruthlessly continued this tradition at Cambridge. At the Old Hall breakfast table each morning I would deliver my latest stool sample update: 'Listen, everyone, I have just had a wonderful bowel movement.' It was disappointing how little they seemed to care. Alas, not every family was like mine.

BREASTS: I'm glad up to a point that I have big breasts. Up to a point, as I say, because there have been various occasions when they got in the way. Before I wore a bra, when I had to run on the hockey field or catch a bus, for example, I nearly knocked myself out. I remember when I went to record my first commercial voice-over with John Wood at his studios in Soho, I was in my little sound booth running through the script and John was alarmed by a resounding bang. 'What the fuck's that?' he cried. I explained that it was the thud of my breasts hitting the table, where for comfort I'd decided to park them. I promised I would try not to repeat that mistake, but given the ever-increasing size of my bosom it has been a perennial problem since, because any obstacle between the microphone and oneself becomes a hazard.

BREXIT: Brexit must be reversed: hopefully in my lifetime, but if not – in yours. Freedom of movement? BOLLOCKS! I want my life back. And my heart bleeds for Britain, particularly for the young. We are part of Europe; the knaves who bamboozled the nation into thinking otherwise will deserve the damning verdict of history, but I won't be there to see it. Their names are David Cameron, Nigel Farage, Boris Johnson, Michael Gove and Jacob Rees-Mogg. We are their victims. They are the instruments of evil. I will NEVER forgive those idiots who voted for this insanity. Don't you dare forgive them, God. They knew exactly what they were doing.

BROADMOOR: My great-grandfather was a crim condemned to seven years' hard labour in Parkhurst but I didn't know this when I started going to the Oxford magistrates' court after school to sit in the public gallery and listen to the cases. Usefully sited next door to the library, where I would pick up my latest batch of books, it was in the courts I could bathe in real-life drama. I was so fascinated that my school magazine predicted my future career was to become a probation officer, not an actress.

At Cambridge's Freshers' Fair, the Social Services Organisation mainly caught my eye because it promised trips to prisons. I wanted to hobnob with crims very much. I signed up immediately. But the visit to Broadmoor, an institution for the criminally insane, sharply widened my acquaintance. It was remarkably unsupervised. We were taken around in a jolly group, and then we were left alone with the inmates. I can remember vividly how many of those incarcerated at Broadmoor looked as mad as snakes. And, of course, we knew that they were nearly all murderers. Our group was taken to the carpentry workshop, full of saws, hammers, drills and screwdrivers – useful weaponry and so close at hand. As usual, I was so caught up in the chatting opportunities that I got left behind. And then suddenly I realised that I was on my own in a room full of sharp objects and convicted killers. I wanted to be polite but I *really* wanted to get away. Smiling warmly, I said, 'Oh, goodness, is that the time? It has been fascinating talking to you, but they've left me behind. I'd better hurry up before I get into trouble.' And I left smartish. Somewhat to my chagrin, my absence had not been noticed by my Social Services team.

BULLIES: To make anyone feel small is a nasty thing to do, because one of the things you realise as you go through life is that everybody is scared inside. If someone speaks to me in an aggressive way, I immediately call it out. 'Who the fuck do you think you are …?' I bellow. 'Don't speak to me like that! I won't have it.' And even worse, if I see somebody mistreating a dog or whipping a horse, I'll shout, 'Stop that right now!' It's very important to stand up to bullies.

BURNING YOUR BOATS: I've burned my boats and there they are, smouldering in public view.

BURTON AND TAYLOR: In February 1966, Richard Burton and Elizabeth Taylor came to perform *Dr Faustus*, by Christopher Marlowe, at the Oxford Playhouse. At that time, they were the biggest stars in the world and the tickets for the show sold out in minutes. My unstoppable friend Mahnaz and I decided to lug two stools down to the Playhouse box office and camp outside all night for returns. At about two in the morning, we noticed a Rolls Royce saloon pull up outside the Randolph Hotel. A couple emerged. It was Burton and Taylor. Imminent sex hung in the air – for them, not for us. The richest and happiest people in the world were about to have a fuck, but then, instead of going straight into the hotel, they walked towards us. Celebrity at close quarters is heady stuff. Somehow the unbelievable appears entirely natural. They were relaxed, enjoying both our delight in them and the absurdity of our waiting all night in the freezing February weather. Here they were, sharing their happiness and letting us into their golden bubble. 'You must be mad,' Burton said. 'Give your names to my friend here at the stage door and join us tomorrow for a drink.' Taylor didn't say much but almost the entire time her violet eyes were smiling. We felt chosen, uplifted – somehow at the centre of the earth. I remember little of the show; just being there was the enchantment. Then we gave our names to the stage door and clustered in a dressing room – an ordinary space made astonishing because *they* were there.

Drinks were served. At some point, I boldly said, 'You really must play *Anna Karenina* together.' Burton looked up, amused. 'You mean, you want her to speak?' In *Dr Faustus*, Elizabeth Taylor was playing the silent role of Helen of Troy, 'the face that launched a thousand ships and burnt the topless towers of Ilium'. Everyone, including her, laughed.

Afterwards Faustus's final speech, suddenly realising it was too late and he was about to be dragged off to Hell, was stuck in my head.

> Ah, Faustus,
> Now hast thou but one bare hour to live,
> And then thou must be damned perpetually!
> Stand still, you ever-moving spheres of Heaven,
> That time may cease, and midnight never come ...
> *O lente, lente, currite noctis equi!* *
> The stars move still, time runs, the clock will strike,
> The Devil will come, and Faustus must be damned.

Burton was speaking it straight out of the heart of his own Faustian bargain – life and happiness for love and celebrity – knowing the sands of his own hourglass were already running out. I've never forgotten it.

BUTTOCKS: I've always been little and fat; that can deceive people into thinking you're a pushover. Well, I'm not. I'm not a Christian; I won't turn the other cheek, unless it's a buttock.

---

* O, run slowly, slowly, horses of the night!

CADBURY'S CARAMEL BUNNY: When, forty-five years ago in 1980, I was offered the voice of the Cadbury's Caramel Rabbit, I was told that 'it's got to be sexy'. To me, a sexy voice is an exhausted voice, of somebody who's had so many orgasms they've hardly got the strength to speak. So, although my normal tones are not like this, by breathing languorously through my lines, I had become known for being able to simulate a guttural groan of multiple orgasm, something that could be possibly helped by the richness of the chocolate being advertised. For the heavy-eyed Bunny, I added a rural, milkmaid drawl, more Oxfordshire than Devon, to be honest:

> Hey, Mr Beaver, why are you beavering around? Haven't you heard of Cadbury's Caramel? See, as the thick Cadbury's milk chocolate melts with that dreamy caramel, you just have to take things really easy. [*The lovestruck beaver has chewed all the way through a tree, ignoring the angry squirrels whose home he has destroyed.*] Looks like somebody else could do with some. Take it easy with Cadbury's Caramel.

Many years later, after my voice had been voted the Third Sexiest in Europe, another actress took up my pail and did a skilful imitation. I'd love to know who it was.

CALLIPYGIAN: I recently discovered a delightful word: 'callipygian'. It means 'possessed of a pleasing bottom', 'having well-shaped buttocks'; from the Ancient Greek, *kallos* = beauty

+ *puge* = buttocks. The synonyms are 'bootylicious', 'bumtastic', 'callipygous' and 'rumpalicious'. (For breasts, the equivalent of 'callipygian', though not a direct equivalent, is 'bathycolpian', from the Greek adjective which means 'bosoms', 'with deep full breasts', used in the Homeric epics for the pretty Trojan ladies in lyric poetry.) 'Callipygian' is a useful word, I should imagine, when admiring a classical statue of some kind, like Michelangelo's *David* – his bottom is pleasant. But the front botty is somewhat disappointing: the world's tiniest penis.

C

CAMEO: One of the recent additions to my life has been the popularisation of social media. It's not *really* social, because it involves long solitary hours spent staring at screens, either large or small, rather than real social intercourse – chatting, gossiping, exchanging ideas and looking into real people's eyes. It's the tool for some people to become billionaires and then control our thoughts, our very means of expressing ourselves. And from that has developed the 'celebrity message': people paying for people they see only on screens to send quite intimate messages on more screens to their friends and people they know and love but prefer to reach through others. I make a lot of money working with one such firm – Cameo, an internet business founded in Chicago in 2016 by Steve Galanis. Generally, I am asked to swear, fart and send cheeky birthday messages. Try as I might, I can't get it across to people that **FARTING** cannot be done to order – wind has its own laws – but should an anal bubble manifest, I allow it full microphone time. Occasionally, I am requested to give someone a pep talk or wish a cancer sufferer better. That is very tough, but I take it seriously and try to offer comfort, give good advice and be real – it seems we are all desperate for authenticity, probably because we are constantly being lied to. I only hope my genuine desire to make people happy, to comfort them in distress and always tell the truth, comes across. Making people laugh is a Good Thing. If I swear, curse or expose my bottom or breasts, what harm am I doing? It's a grim enough world, let's be kind to one another, and to hell with the cunts who try to deceive and mislead us.

CAMILLA: I was invited to perform some Dickens characters at the Queen's Reading Room, Camilla's annual literary festival at Hampton Court. Before the show, there was a reception. It was too far for this old cripple to walk, and I was ferried through miles of corridors of amazing Holbein portraits and tapestries to the Great Hall in my wheelchair. Shakespeare and his company had performed *A Midsummer's Night's Dream* for Elizabeth I in this room. Now it was filled with writers and actors, and a smiling blonde figure, unflanked by bodyguards: Camilla.

Determined to have a better conversation with this queen than I had had with her frostier mother-in-law (see **QUIET, BE**), I stepped forward to shake the royal hand. I was so delighted to see her coming toward me, beaming away, that, overawed by the occasion, I decided to curtsy. But, then, on the way down, I wobbled precariously and, without thinking, grabbed at Camilla's outstretched hand. The full force of my desperate grip fastened mercilessly on the queen, pulling her down with me – and I am no lightweight. My only thought was not to fall. A horrifying vision of our descent to the floor flashed before my eyes. Camilla flailing on top of me, in her smart dress, while I waved my legs in the air, surrounded by the frozen faces of the literary great and good. But then, somehow, without assistance, Camilla managed to steady both me and herself, and the look on her kind face as she righted me was one of genuine concern, rather than irritation. A cat can look at a queen, yes, but it shouldn't capsize her.

C

CARPE DIEM: My motto in life, which I always wrote in autograph albums, has always been *Carpe Diem*: Seize the Day. Don't waste a second, plunge into life and savour every moment. It's over in a trice; this is not a dress rehearsal: this is it! My other meme of choice was 'Only Connect' from E. M. Forster. And that's the very first time I've ever used the word 'meme'.

CAST YOUR BREAD ON THE WATERS AND IT WILL COME BACK SANDWICHES: Mummy always said this. What I think it means is: don't hold on to safe ideas. Be daring and generous and you will be rewarded. Mummy was naturally a generous person; Daddy was not. And I feel battling within me the twin qualities of meanness and generosity bestowed on me by the lifestyles of my parents. I yield to one and then the other – it's a struggle. I see Daddy turning off the lights and Mummy sharing a tangerine, pushing it into her carer's hand with her one unparalysed one. 'Pouff I want,' she urges unintelligibly, but meaning 'Do have a tangerine, darling – it's all I can give you.'

CENTIMORGAN: I get emails every day from people who think we're related, saying 'We share some centimorgans' – a centimorgan is a particle of a DNA chain.* At first, I thought it denoted a weighty preponderance of Welsh in my genes. No such luck, but I did find an unknown cousin through this method.

CHARISMA: A particular type of charisma – or 'manipulative charm' – has been passed down through generations of my family. Some people have it and some do not. My great-grandfather had it, my mother certainly did, and so do I. When you have it, you know you have it, and you must be very careful not to misuse your power. My great-grandfather did misuse it, and most likely my grandfather did too, because everybody seemed to adore him uncritically, despite his unfaithfulness to Grandma.

CHEESECAKE: Life is like cheesecake: you always want another slice.

CHILDREN: I'd never be cruel to a child, but best keep them away from me, if possible. And babies are best left at home. I'm happy once children can talk, and I do enjoy discovering (and scaring) my friends' grandchildren. But never in Business Class, please.

---

*Here's a useful link which will show you whether it's worth replying to the putative cousin: https://www.familysearch.org/en/blog/cousin-chart

CHRISTIANITY: We only have one life. That's the terrible truth. I don't believe in reincarnation. I don't believe that I'll come back as Princess Margaret or a baby elephant. I believe that I'm here and now and I must make it work and do the best I can. One of the problems with Christianity is that they think they get a second chance and they think that there's life up there in heaven. Bollocks! Do it now, do it here and love yourself a little ... not *too* much, but a little.

C

CHRISTMAS: When I was little, I once asked for a Christmas tree. 'Absolutely not,' Daddy responded. He was right and now I hate Christmas as much as he did. It is imposed commercialism under the guise of religious fervour, full of people buying presents for people they don't like with money they don't have. I use my Jewishness as an excuse for avoiding it (just as I successfully avoid Jehovah's Witnesses), even though I'm not a believer.

COCK-SUCKING: It's what Jewish girls have always done. You don't get pregnant, you get POPULAR! It doesn't need a lot of space and remarkably little time! One evening, late after rehearsals, I was in the Newnham bike shed sucking someone off. And Lesley Cook, my moral tutor, was parking her bike and she saw me. She didn't see the bloke as he was in the shadows, but she saw me bending down over something and said, 'Goodnight, Miriam.' 'Goo' 'ight, 'iss 'ook,' came my polite reply, my usually clear diction muddied as my mouth was full of cock.

COFFIN: I have tried out a coffin TWICE. Once in a film, acting with a much older actress who was meant to get into it but couldn't face it, so I jumped in with gay abandon. And once for TV, where I was delighted to discover that the Coffin Club in Hastings has one that you can order – one size fits all. As I'm a bit fat, I had to get into it quite gingerly. And I just about fitted. Until, of course, the lid had to be put on … No easy business, as I had to hold down my tits to stop them from thrusting off the lid. I think it's still waiting for me in Hastings. Very plain – it's just got a Star of David on it, to acknowledge my Jewishness. But death should be an unvarnished business, I think.

COMEDY: My secret weapon against bullies has always been comedy. There's something about my face and my body which makes people laugh. I've always known that. From the earliest days at school, I found out that if you make people laugh, they will let you do almost anything. I scored goals at hockey, I made friends. Comedy is so much more than a TV department.

CONFIDANTE: One of my greatest strengths is that I have no secrets. It so happens that many of the confidences shared with me are from elderly women who did have a secret, who have become lesbians in later life. Some of these are revelations I could have told them years ago, but others are freshly minted. Their surprise at the fact that a cunt-on-cunt situation can be exquisite is both a source of delight and great hilarity to me. Better late than never, I always say. And if you think that the lesbian libido is diminished by age, think again. You go into an old people's home (average population 95 per cent female!) at your own risk.

CONFIDENCE: I know I seem very confident but inside, let me assure you, I'm not. Everyone is afraid, we all feel the terror of failure, of being overlooked, of being worthless; even Elton John – maybe not Barbra Streisand. Unless you're Putin, Trump or Netanyahu, you are a decent human being and should try to feel good in yourself. Look in the mirror and say, 'I've never killed anybody. I've never murdered anybody. I've never damaged anybody.' And let that carry you out of the door. Take a deep breath and say to yourself 'I MATTER!' as you enter the room.

C

CONVERSATION: Some people think of conversation as a tug of war, or would do anything to avoid starting one. Not I! My objective on a walk in the park is always to focus on the bench with someone on it and go and talk to them. The joy of being on an aeroplane is having a potential new friend firmly belted into the neighbouring seat. Rest assured I can take a hint. If you firmly put your headphones on I won't bother you but I will be sad at the opportunity missed.

I regard everyone as a new friend – I always have. There's no such thing as a boring person. Once you've talked to someone, they become interesting. Some people use pets as an opening gambit – I prefer 'Why did you buy that scarf?' or that sort of thing. The way to start a conversation is to focus on the other person, and they usually will respond. Then you're off and no subject is off limits, the more contentious the better.

CORPSING is how actors refer to the fits of uncontrollable giggles that overcome them, even Judi Dench (especially Judi Dench!), when something untoward happens on stage and you fall out of character. The first night of Eugene O'Neill's *Long Day's Journey into Night* at the ADC Theatre in Cambridge provided one of my worst corpses. I was playing Mary Cavan Tyrone. The third act begins with a stage direction:

> Dusk is gathering in the living room, an early dusk due to the fog which has rolled in from the Sound and is like a white curtain drawn down outside the windows.

In order to achieve this effect, the stage management had been working very hard in the wings during the interval, using the fog machine. They were surprisingly efficient.

When the curtain rose, I was onstage with Cathleen, the servant girl. But I couldn't see her, she couldn't see me, and the audience couldn't see either of us – though I could hear the front row, coughing hard. My first line is: 'That foghorn! Isn't it awful, Cathleen?' In my anxiety, I said instead, 'The fog is thick tonight, Cathleen.' There was a roar of agreement from the audience, and laughter which lasted a good minute, accompanied by clapping and foot-stamping. Very hard to keep your voice straight in the circumstances.

COSTUME DRAMA: Nineteenth-century American high society was a complicated new world to recreate, and for *The Age of Innocence*, Martin Scorsese and his extended crew were grimly determined to get every aspect of their production spot-on. It was the end of an extremely long and hot day. Since 6 a.m., the crew had watched a long succession of actors parade across the podium for hair and make-up approval. Actor followed actor and hour followed hour. I was the very last one, facing an exhausted workforce. By now their faces were polite, but lined with fatigue. I felt it was my duty to raise their spirits.

'It's Miriam Margolyes playing Mrs Mingott,' I said. 'And you deserve these.'

And without further ado, I pulled up my maroon 'Dickens' Universe' sweatshirt, and there they were, my proud and thrusting breasts, naked and unashamed. Martin Scorsese and the assembled crew were initially stunned into a dazed silence and then broke into roars of laughter. That was a costume they weren't expecting. Scorsese has never forgotten it. Many years later, he said to me, 'I remember that hair and make-up parade most particularly.'

CRACKED ON SOMEONE, BEING: At school I used to have huge pashes on people; we called it being 'cracked'. The violence of the language is completely appropriate, as this was much worse than a mere 'crush' – it was a pulverising experience. I even wrote a little essay in 1954 on the subject for the Oxford High School magazine entitled 'People I Have Been Cracked On (or rather, People On Whom I Have Been Cracked)'. Some are still my friends, the pash has been replaced by warm friendship. More restful.

CRISPS: A lot of my life is spent thinking about crisps and eating crisps and afterwards hating myself for eating crisps. It's just not worth it. Or it wouldn't be if crisps weren't so delicious.

CUNT: I love words, and the word 'cunt' is the linguistic equivalent of opening a bottle of smelling salts. A cunt is a powerful and beautiful thing. 'She has a cunt like a cathedral' was a common term of abuse when I was at Cambridge. You will never hear that from me. For me, a cunt *is* a cathedral.

CUNT-FACE: 'Cunt-face' is my rude word of choice; it's unisexually employed, but I haven't found a gesture to indicate an enormous vagina, which would be the equivalent insult for a woman. Odd that size matters so much – women must be small in that area; men, big.

There is an undeniable pleasure in seeing the shock, sometimes disgust, on faces when I shout foul language at strangers, often in the car. 'CUNT-FACE!' I shriek through the open window at the offending driver, usually male, who tries to cut me up, beat me to the get-away or threatens me from behind. And I gleefully represent their tiny appendage with thumb and forefinger, to reinforce my rage and contempt.

CURIOSITY: My life has always been motivated by violent and uncontrollable curiosity – I don't just want to know who someone is. I want to know everything about them. Their hopes, their dreams, everything that makes them tick. And I want to know it now. (See also **DOCUMENTARIAN**.)

DADDY: Dr Joseph Margolyes was born in the Gorbals, Glasgow, on 29 January 1899, and died in Clapham, London, on 10 February 1995. I always called him Daddy; Mummy called him Joe. He was below average height, of slender build, with a fine head of black hair, a small moustache, large brown eyes and a sweet smile. He was of a nervous disposition, afraid of social challenge, of new situations, of unspecified outcomes. All his life, women looked after him. Money enabled me to care for him as he faced widowerhood, old age and ultimately dementia. He was capable of great love and great meanness. He was a superb and conscientious doctor, a man of honour and decency, a devout Jew but never a Zionist. I wish I could have been the daughter he longed for. I honour his memory.

DAME, NOTHING LIKE A: Sometimes people say, 'You ought to be a Dame.' My response is, 'Darling, I don't think I'm good enough.' Of course, I would have loved to be Damed – and I must confess to a squidge of rage when I see that this, that or the other person has been made one – and I haven't. It's obvious who the Great Dames are – they most definitely deserve their honours.

In the 2004 film *Ladies in Lavender*, I was acting with Dames Judi Dench and Maggie Smith. They remained the Ladies while I played their aged retainer, Dorcas, comically obsessed with root vegetables and shoes being cleaned properly. We three actresses shared a sitting-out space. Judi knitted or crocheted; Maggie did the crossword. They were always welcoming, but I felt intimidated, desperately reaching for increasingly unnecessary topics to keep the conversation going. My worst blunder came when I said brightly, 'Shall we talk about acting?' After a beat of disbelief, they lowered their knitting and crosswords simultaneously and stared at me. 'No, let's NOT!' said Maggie firmly. The memory of that moment still makes my toes curl almost twenty years on.

DARLINGS, MURDER YOUR: Peter Hall, for whom I had the joy of working four times, once said to me, 'Murder your darlings' – which means, when you think you're being brilliant, that's when you should stop. It's the best piece of advice I've ever been given, in acting or otherwise. Nothing good can come from smugness.

DEATH: When you're young, you never think about death. You just think about your next fuck. Now I think about death a lot. Every morning when I get up, I think, 'Hmmm, another day.' I can't help but be aware that the amount of time ahead of me is less than the time behind. But I'm still ducking and diving. I'm still open to new experiences. However, I'm conscious that there is no light at the end of this particular tunnel. *Now* is the moment that counts. You've got to *carpe* that *diem*. It's a solemn subject and requires thought and preparation. If only we knew WHEN. And HOW. I long for an easy death, without pain and incontinence. I'd prefer to be at home, rather than be felled in the street and helped into an ambulance by well-meaning strangers. I wonder how I'll be remembered, talked about, possibly reviled. It's hard not to have FOMO that things will go on without me – because they will. It's time to stop wallowing and get on with living.

DENTIST: I played the dental nurse-cum-punchbag in *Little Shop of Horrors* (1986) to Steve Martin's psychopathic dentist. During my only musical number ('Dentist!') I was hit all day by doors opening in my face; repeatedly punched, slapped and knocked down by an unlovely and unapologetic Steve Martin – perhaps he was method acting – and came home grumpy with a splitting headache. Let it not be said that I have never suffered in the name of Art.

DIAMOND: This is the best story my father ever told me. There's such emotion behind it: great love and desperation. I used to tell it in my show *The Importance of Being Miriam*. Every night on stage, it made me cry, and in bringing to life a real moment in my family history, I felt close again to my father.

The story takes place in Glasgow, where Daddy was born and brought up, the eldest of four children. In 1917, one morning at breakfast, his call-up papers arrived, summoning him to join the 4th Battalion, Highland Light Infantry, and prepare to leave for France. The First World War was called the Great War but it was great only in the numbers killed. The average life expectancy of a young officer in 1917 was six weeks. My grandfather was a serious, decent man who had worked his way up from selling little pieces of costume jewellery to the miners' wives in the Lowlands, and finally ended up quite wealthy, with a wholesale jewellery shop in St Enoch's Square. When he saw the call-up papers, he immediately realised that they were a death sentence and that his beloved son could die in the killing fields of Flanders like all the other young men he'd known.

He immediately made an appointment with the Commanding Officer of the Battalion in the regimental headquarters. But on the way he visited the warehouse of his shop.

Imagine a slight, black-haired, Jewish man in a business suit, forty-three years old, knocking at the Commanding Officer's door.

'Come in.'

When Grandpa Margolyes entered, he saw a vigorous officer in full military uniform seated behind a desk. 'What can I do for you?' he said briskly. He did not offer my grandfather a seat.

Grandpa replied in broken, heavily accented English; he was nervous but polite. 'First of all, I want to thank you for the kindness of seeing me today. I know how busy you are with many vital things to do, but my need to have this interview with you is very great. Today, Joseph, my eldest child, received his call-up papers to join your regiment in France. He is just eighteen and has won a scholarship to study medicine at Glasgow University, the first member of our family to have such an opportunity. You know – and I know – how short is the life of a young soldier in Flanders; in six weeks he will be dead. He is a fine young man, a good son, he will make a good doctor and save many lives. I ask you to remove his name from the draft. But I cannot do this without giving you something in return. The most valuable thing I have – apart from my son – is *this*.' He put his hand into the pocket of his suit and took something from it. He stretched out his arm and opened his hand; there in his palm was a large diamond. 'This diamond is almost flawless; it is the finest in my warehouse. I beg you to take it in exchange for the life of my son. Please. Take it – please.'

The diamond glinted in his palm.

At that point, I used to stop the story and asked the audience what they thought would happen. Many thought it inconceivable that a Scottish officer could ever be bribed. They were wrong. He took the diamond and Daddy's name was taken off the draft. He went on to university and became an excellent doctor. Yes – it was bribery, but I'm proud that my grandfather was prepared to risk his good name and his livelihood to save his son's life. After all, it's why I am here to tell the tale.

DICAPRIO, LEONARDO: Everyone on the set of *Romeo + Juliet* fell head over heels for Leo, from Baz Luhrmann to Claire Danes. I liked him tremendously and admired his work, but I was immune to his groin charms. And I think he might have found that refreshing. Well, he preferred me as a shopping companion. We'd spend hours going through the markets together – I don't know that I've ever had such fun. He had a real taste for bling. Now he's grown into a fine actor but, back then, he was just a handsome boy who didn't always wash; he was quite smelly in that male way some young men are. Sometimes he wore a dress. I said to him, 'Leo, I think you're gay.' He burst out laughing and said, 'No, I'm not, Miriam. I'm really *not* gay.' I insisted, 'I think you'll find you are.' But I was wrong. He did it to be talked about – much as I did when I smoked my pipe at Cambridge.

DICK: On certain days, the Oxford High School sports pavilion was let out to a boys' school and once, I happened to walk past the open door and I saw a completely naked man in profile cross to the showers – with his dick sticking out in front. I think that was probably the first time I'd ever seen an erect penis, and I didn't like it. And I never have.

DICKENS, CHARLES: In many ways, this has been the hardest entry of the book to write, because my passion for the man and his writings inflames me but my rage at his faults still burns. He was wicked and loveable and capricious and gifted beyond belief. He was a mass of contradictions – complicated and pitiful, big-hearted and vindictive, one of the greatest geniuses who ever lived, an adulterer and a family man, a drunk, a dandy and yet someone who never forgot the poverty of his youth.

I met him first when I was eleven through the pages of *Oliver Twist*; and I am still reading his letters (he wrote over 14,000) at eighty-four. Reading his novel, I felt I was Oliver, then Nancy, then Fagin. The drama and the humanity pulled me in. Dickens wanted to be an actor, he would read all his books aloud to himself in a mirror, playing all the characters; Helen Mirren would definitely disapprove.

In 1986, my dear friend, Sonia Fraser and I decided to concoct an entertainment, *Dickens' Women*, which coupled telling the story of his life *and* playing all the women's parts I could manage (and a few men!). I particularly love Mrs **GAMP**, the midwife based on a real midwife who had once, obviously blind drunk, attended his wife, Catherine, 'leave the bottle on the Chimley piece and don't ask me to take none, but let me put my lips to it when I am so dispoged' and the unforgettable Miss **HAVISHAM** from *Great Expectations*, whose bitter voice I believe to be Dickens himself, following the break-up of his marriage. 'I'll tell you what real love is. It is blind devotion, unquestioning self-humiliation, utter submission, trust and belief against yourself and against the whole world, giving up your whole heart and soul to the smiter — as I did!'

We took our show round the world and from Madras to Hollywood, from Tel Aviv to Vancouver, his magic worked. It still works; I've played the Edinburgh Fringe for the last two years, with amorous Mr Bumble from *Oliver Twist*, 'Mrs Corney, ma'am, I mean to say this, ma'am, that any cat, or kitten that could live with you, ma'am, and not be fond of its home, must be an ass, ma'am', and pathetic Miss Flite from *Bleak House*, 'I am sorry I cannot offer chocolate. I expect a judgement shortly and shall then place my establishment on a superior footing. At present, I don't mind confessing (in strict confidence), that I sometimes find it difficult to keep up a genteel appearance. I have felt the cold here. I have felt something sharper than cold. It matters very little. Pray excuse the introduction of such mean topics.' I can't let go of any of them.

Dickens was born a Georgian in 1812, into the violent, jolly, peripatetic world he describes in his first novel, *The Pickwick Papers*, and died in 1870, an exhausted, depressed husk, only fifty-eight, leaving the mistress he'd had to hide, a broken family and fifteen novels, five novellas and hundreds of short stories containing the most vivid, brilliant descriptions of the nineteenth century. Though angry and disappointed at every new terrible thing I find out about the man, I can only beg you to read or re-read his works and your deepest soul will be refreshed and enchanted, just as mine still is.

DIE, ALWAYS SAY: People are embarrassed by death. They say 'pass away' instead of 'die'. But I prefer to face Death head-on; call it like it is; face reality and deal with it. Some people cannot do this and it infuriates me. When will we ever grow up?

DIETING: I have never been asked to lose weight for a part, but I have always wanted to be slimmer, so I have often gone on diets and tried various slimming treatments over the years. I went to Tyringham Hall in Newport Pagnell back in the seventies, then a naturopathic health farm in a Grade I listed stately home designed by Sir John Soane. Various water treatments including ice-cold power showers, glacial plunge pools, cold-towel wraps and a sauna were on offer. I had read that in Scandinavia, after their sauna, people would go outside and cover themselves in fresh snow. So, on one particularly icy day, after I'd heated myself up to a boil in their sauna, I ran out buck-naked and rolled about on the thickly snow-carpeted lawns at the front of the mansion. Suitably invigorated and tingling pink all over, I stood up to face the interested gazes of a party of visitors being shown around by Sidney Rose-Neil, the director of Tyringham. He said to me rather curtly, 'Can I see you later?' When I went to his office, he said, 'I quite understand that you wanted to experience the sauna, but please don't go cavorting in the snow again, because the sight of a naked Miriam Margolyes is not something all our visitors may appreciate.'

DIETRICH, MARLENE: Marlene Dietrich came to Britain to do a show at the Golders Green Hippodrome. After the show, I queued outside the stage door with all the other fans until finally she came out looking impossibly glamorous. Then she climbed onto the roof of the car that had come to fetch her and sat and talked to us for over an hour. She clearly enjoyed our adulation and flirted and teased and joked until the years fell away from her and you could have sworn she was a young girl again, making eyes at all of us. She was utterly compelling. I called out, 'Du warst wunderbar.' That got her attention. She smiled delightedly. 'Sprichst du Deutsch?' Then she leaned down, cupped my face in her hands and kissed me.

DIRECT, ALWAYS BE: People have remarked that I possess a childlike quality. I'm not sure that they always mean it in a positive way. In my communication with others, I never ask for permission. I state what is on my mind, pungently but politely. And they, in return, must tell me truthfully what is on their mind. I hope I am good at receiving the blunt truth from my friends – it is the better way.

DIRECTION can be a revelation or a total waste of time. For example, if a director says, 'Be an ostrich,' or 'Be more brown' (that was actually said to me), I know it's not going to work. I belong to a more conventional school of acting; I'm with Noël Coward, who said, 'Learn your lines and don't bump into the furniture.' If you bring your full *energy* to the rehearsal room, if you open yourself to the director, and if they are wise and intellectually energetic, a wonderful fusion of imaginations can result.

DISCIPLINE: I'm not sure this is a talent, but I need it more than any other. I have talent; I need discipline to harness and organise it. I am lazy, I procrastinate, I allow myself to fritter away the most precious thing there is – time! What a pity.

'DO YOU LIKE ME?': When I asked Liz Hodgkin, still one of my closest friends, what I was like at school, she said I was always asking: 'Do you like me?' I desperately wanted to be liked. I'd do almost anything to be liked. I haven't changed.

'DOCTOR IN THE HOUSE, IS THERE A?': I have only once broken character. I was giving my one-woman show *Dickens' Women* at the Hampstead Theatre Club, when a continuing snorting and growling sound became evident in the back stalls. It grew in volume and intensity. The audience was becoming restive and clearly anxious. Finally, I held up my hand, came to the front of the stage and said: 'Is there a doctor in the house?' And, of course, because it was Hampstead, nearly everybody stood up. A lady in the audience was having an epileptic fit; she couldn't have had it in a better place. Several doctors attended her, the show resumed and I'm pleased to say she fully recovered.

DOCUMENTARIAN: Documentaries give me such a wonderful opportunity to engage fully, talking, questioning, learning. I now realise I've always been a documentarian; it's just another word for Nosy Parker. As soon as I've met people, I've always asked them everything I could. Age has only increased my curiosity and the urgency of satisfying it. No one is safe now I have a mobility-scooter and I've actually found being short is rather a help. I've had to get used to looking up into nostrils, rather than straight into eyes. But people find it easier to confide in someone short. Everyone likes feeling interesting, and amazingly, when you ask the right questions, most people really are.

DOGS: My family always had a dog and I long for one, but my peripatetic life prohibits such a thing. Bonnie, my first dog was an English Springer Spaniel of intense nobility. My second a scoundrel Scottish Border Collie, called Whiskey. I always speak to dogs I meet in the street; I long for their snuffles and tail-wags.

DOLLY FART-ON: This is one of my favourite and most requested stories: my own version of *Gone With the Wind*, with Graham Norton as a reluctant Rhett Butler, Wembley Stadium standing in for Tara, myself channelling an uncorseted Vivien Leigh and straining to hold in the gathering sulphur clouds.

We'd been invited to a meet-and-greet moment after Dolly Parton's glittering concert. I hadn't realised that we would be joining a queue of about 150 people and I could feel a fart gathering as the moments passed. I held it in for a *long* time. But the moment when I knew I'd reached the end of The Holding, my fart finally burst forth like a bullet from Big Bertha, the wartime gun. It exploded gloriously with such a gigantic boom I fear the security guards thought it might have been a terrorist attack.

Inevitably, the architecture of the tunnel we were waiting in helped to prolong and amplify my wind break. It must have lasted about four seconds – that's quite long for a fart. The entire queue tottered in shock; Graham, a slight figure, trembled and nearly fell in its wake. Normally I would have said 'That's better' but this time I was in a paroxysm of embarrassment. At last, it ended – no one moved or spoke … and then an eruption of laughter and relief swept through the tunnel. No one who was there has ever forgotten it, especially Graham, who was both shaken and stirred by the experience.

DON'T GIVE UP: Rejection is always a bitter pill. I cannot sweeten the moment for you, it hurts like hell. But if you're chasing any dream, you have to be able to swallow hard and continue. Don't allow yourself to be deflected, don't let puny naysayers win the day. Dig into the deepest part of yourself – the *pupik*, as we say in Yiddish; Gentiles translate it rather weakly as 'the belly-button', but I call it 'the inner you', the part no one can reach or damage – and rise again.

D

DREAMS: I find conversations about dreams unspeakably boring. I don't remember my dreams. And if I had interesting dreams, I'd fucking well not tell them to you! They're private. Dreams are people's subconscious, best left alone.

DYKE: I've never been a predatory dyke. I just can't reach, for one thing.

EDINBURGH TATTOO: I love this memory because no one ever believes it, but I promise you, it's quite true. I was walking home after midnight through the Meadows, after performing in a show on the Edinburgh Fringe, when I heard a rustling above me (I'm so short, almost everything is above me, actually). I looked up and in one of the trees, the moonlight revealed a young man nestling on one of the branches. He was in military uniform, vigorously masturbating. I watched him for a moment, just to make sure I had fully grasped the situation. I felt concerned for him, perched as he was, using one hand to maintain his balance, the other to maintain his erection. I asked, perhaps unnecessarily, 'What on earth are you *doing*?' as his activity was not in question, although it was dark and I wasn't, so to speak, right on top of things. I find starting a conversation nearly always reduces tension.

'What is your occupation?' He replied, 'I'm a soldier.' I continued, 'In the Military Tattoo?' 'Yes,' came the reply. That clinched my resolve. I called up firmly, 'Come down at once.' He clambered down. I wasn't afraid, I was truly concerned, and felt that although the Meadows were totally deserted, he was in more danger than I was. 'What's the matter with you?' I said. 'You know you can get into dreadful trouble doing what you're doing? You could destroy your career. What rank are you?' I think he said he was a corporal. I said, 'Now look, I will help you out with this one, but you must go straight home afterwards and remember you are a soldier. You'll get into a lot of trouble if anyone catches you up a tree doing that again. Or indeed anywhere.' I then gave him a helping hand, so to speak, and off he went. He seemed charming; he was quite surprised and I must also say, grateful.

But no – there's more! I didn't say this when I told the story on *The Graham Norton Show*, because I thought it might brand me as a sex maniac. But after the soldier had said cheerio (it only took about eight minutes as he was already halfway to happiness), I was calmly wiping my hand on the grass when I heard someone saying, 'Miriam, do you remember me?' I turned around, and sitting on the bench nearby was a sweet boy I'd known in Oxford, a Nigerian called Winston. He said a bit cheekily, 'I saw how you helped that young man. What about me?' Well, I didn't want to be accused of discrimination and I knew and liked Winston, although our relationship had never been quite so intimate before. I felt he had a point (quite a large one actually) so I reapplied myself to the now familiar task. We were both seated I recall, which was good, as this episode took longer. After a satisfactory climax, Winston also popped home and THEN, Reader ... Act Three began! I hadn't noticed, such was my concentration on the job in hand, but another gentleman had been observing this activity and very politely asked if I would be similarly charitable to him before I got home. It would have been churlish to refuse, so it turned out that night I killed three birds for the price of one. I felt happy, they felt satisfied; truly, what was the harm? No animals were hurt in the process.

EDWARD VII's WEIGHING MACHINE: Driving up to Sandringham enables the visitor to observe the perfect lawns, the pristine pointing, the superb flower beds. I was ushered into the large reception room, laid for tea for myself and eighteen guests. After about half an hour or so, Charles and Camilla joined us, and the prince (as he then still was) went in turn to every single person and welcomed them. When he came to me, I got a hug, then he said, 'There's something I want to show you. Here, come with me.' I followed him back to the porch entrance at the top of the stairs, and saw a curious chair. It was a big brown leather chair, but it wobbled – it seemed not to be properly stable on the ground. Prince Charles said, 'I want you to have a look at that. What do you think it is?' I said, 'Well, it looks like a big fireside seat, or a sofa, or something.' 'No, he said. 'It's a weighing machine.' I was flummoxed and a bit anxious, in case I was going to be publicly exposed as the Fattest Guest that weekend. Prince Charles explained that when Edward VII, his great-great-grandfather, gave his house parties, he would weigh each of his guests when they arrived and then he would weigh them again when they left: and if they hadn't put on weight during their stay, he felt that he had failed as a host. He showed me the original weighing book with all the famous people, dates and weights noted alongside. 'What a terrifying thing to see as a guest!' I said. 'I hope you're not thinking of weighing me!' The prince laughed. 'No', he said, 'but isn't it a wonderful insight into the way they did things then?'

ELEPHANT ETHEL: I have played many whores, prostitutes and ladies of the night. In 1977, when I was cast as Elephant Ethel in *Stand Up, Virgin Soldiers*, I was thirty-six years old, not doing very well as an actress, had found my sexuality and was ready to peddle filth if it got me a job. (Query: have I changed *at all*?) In those days the idea of pretending to be another race as shameful hadn't filtered through to Equity members yet. No one then blamed an actress for racial insensitivity or cultural appropriation. I much enjoyed the fun of a transformation from a fat, plain young Jewess into a curvy, slit-eyed Asian whore. Ninety minutes in make-up, fish-scales at the side of my eyes to drag them upwards into an Asian slant, very heavy red lips and *two* wigs, one on top of the other, tits corralled under my chins and the tightest of revealing costumes. And the fact that the crew adored Ethel the tart, and completely ignored Miriam the actress, spurred me on to more hip-rolling and breast-exposing gyrations as I made my way to set. Would I do it now? Of course not! But there is a part of me which regrets that I can never be an Asian sex-goddess again!

ELEPHANTS: As a child I often took part in poetry reading competitions and I have to admit that I often won. This was a particular favourite of mine:

The Elephant
by Herbert Asquith

Here comes the elephant
Swaying along
With his cargo of children
All singing a song:
To the tinkle of laughter
He goes on his way,
And his cargo of children
Have crowned him with May.
His legs are in leather
And padded his toes;
He can root up an oak
With a whisk of his nose:
With a wave of his trunk
And a turn of his chin
He can pull down a house,
Or pick up a pin.
Beneath his grey forehead
A little eye peers!
Of what is he thinking
Between those wide ears?
Of what does he think?
If he wished to tease,
He could twirl his keeper

E

Over the trees:
If he were not kind,
He could play cup and ball
With Robert and Helen
And Uncle Paul:
But that grey forehead,
Those crinkled ears,
Have learned to be kind
In a hundred years!
And so with the children
He goes on his way
To the tinkle of laughter
And crowned with the May.

I've always been fat; I've sometimes even been referred to as 'the elephant in the room'. I grew accustomed to watching the growing horror in the eyes of my fellow air-passengers as they realised I was to be their Middle Seat. At least money now cushions me from that humiliation – it's Biz Class henceforth till the end.

But my own size has given me a love of elephants, which I've never lost. Even as a kid, I loved them, I have a photo of me at the Zoo on top of one. I loved circuses before I realised how cruel they were. I now support a fine organisation in Kenya called the Sheldrick Wildlife Trust, which takes care of elephants in the wild, rescuing orphans and rearing them to adulthood. Elephants

are amazing animals, long-lived, with loving hearts, affectionate natures, of immense strength and high intelligence. Under constant threat from poachers for their ivory, they need our help to survive. I have adopted three and strongly urge you to do the same. It's my dream to go to Kenya one day with a film crew and meet my adoptees.

When I went to India for the first time, an elephant walked past my hotel as I was having breakfast. I rushed out, clutching an apple and finally caught up with the strolling giant and gave him the apple, marvelling as his trunk found my hand and ever so gently, with a rippling movement, grasped the apple. His eyes took me in, entirely benevolently. We humans have a long way to go to match the sweetness of an elephant.

ELOCUTION: Mummy and Daddy were determined their only child should have every advantage, and consequently I was taught elocution by Miss Mary Plowman. She was an eccentric but loveable woman, who had whiskers and (like my mother) always wore a cape. She suffered from narcolepsy and would fall asleep quite suddenly in the middle of a diphthong. She taught me about diphthongs and triphthongs and iambic pentameters and diaphragmatic intercostal breathing and the value of vowels and consonants. In my occasional masterclasses to drama students, I quote Miss Plowman: 'Remember, vowels carry the emotion in a word – consonants carry the sense.' I enjoyed her lessons;

she made me conscious of 'lips, tongue and teeth'. And breathing was, of course, VITAL. 'Oddi-orri, oddi-orri,' she would make me repeat very fast. 'Breath is the material of which voice is made.'

I don't entirely approve of the concept of elocution. We should judge people according to the purity of their *morals*: the purity of their vowels is neither here nor there. And it's a pity to iron out the rich variety of accents available in the British Isles. We shouldn't all sound the same. Therefore, in some ways I regret that my vowels are pure – because they are: I doubt you'll hear a purer vowel in Equity.

E

EMBONPOINT: Like every woman blessed with embonpoint, I have often experienced my breasts being spoken to rather than my face. All the men (and women too) I've ever known sexually have wanted to fondle and play with them. It was Major Harding (aptly named), a retired Army officer living in North Oxford, who taught me one favourite amatory technique: my breasts were perfect for holding an erect penis, exerting a little friction until the desired ejaculation took place. I felt my repertoire of love really increased under his kindly instruction. I wanted to please and I did – often. I felt in control of everything and was never in danger. Army discipline is sometimes to be admired. So, at Cambridge and beyond, I found that to squeeze a penis between my globes of glory always resulted in cries of 'Encore!'

EMOTION: I can reach my emotions easily, I don't have to dig deep for them. Perhaps it's because of my Jewish heritage that I have emotions readily available just below the surface; tears and laughter and rage and delight can be summoned for the character I'm playing. Some may call me a 'drama queen'. 'I think, therefore I am' – yes, of course. But surely we also need: 'I *feel*, therefore I'm *alive*'.

ESCOBAR, MIRIAM: See **WHITE SNIFFS OF DOVER**.

EXERCISE: I used to swim forty lengths every day but now no longer. A Pilates instructor used to come to my house in London and we'd do it in my kitchen, but now I make excuses and say that I don't have time. My exercise bike sits there, rusting away. It's feeble; I know I must or I'll die. And of course, it would help with my mobility – indeed, with everything. The truth is that I just can't bear exercise.

EYES: If you're fat, people tell you, 'Oh, you've got lovely eyes,' as if that more than makes up for it. Which it doesn't, but it doesn't mean I'm not proud of my dark brown eyes. Mummy used to say, 'Eyes are the window of the soul.' And they are.

Heather has blue eyes. Daddy's were dark brown. He was handsome when he was young, but I don't think he ever knew

that he was handsome. He never thought about things like that. And Mummy's were a brilliant bright blue. Icy. When she got angry, her eyes fixed you and were like points of fire. Grandpa Walters's eyes were blue too. He was the seductive one, the conjuror.

E

FACE: I've come to terms with the fact that my body is not a pretty sight. It's my own fault – I've eaten too much all my life, and now the fat intends to stay, settled in for the duration. I hope people concentrate on my face, which is warm, friendly and, although lined, has a girlish aspect which can be quite charming.

FAGIN: During a BBC live radio show from the Edinburgh Fringe Festival, I was asked by Kirsty Wark which Dickens character stuck in my head most as a child. I replied, truthfully, 'Fagin, without question; described as "Jewish and vile".'
Take these lines from *Oliver Twist*:

> In short, the wily old Jew had the boy in his toils. Having prepared his mind, by solitude and gloom, to prefer any society to the companionship of his own sad thoughts in such a dreary place, he was now slowly instilling into his soul the poison which he hoped would blacken it, and change its hue for ever.

I read that when I was eleven in 1952, only seven years after a terrible war, in which among many millions who died were members of my family, gassed in Treblinka. No one spoke of Jews then in this way; they couldn't. I knew I was Jewish; I loved being Jewish. All the Jews I knew in 1952 were clever, told jokes well, cooked superbly and were kind. But Dickens was accurately reflecting both his personal and the contemporary national animosities on the page; his genius was to make evil funny and slightly ridiculous, and then the reader, all unaware, cheers along at the downfall of the Jew. English literature, my great love, is full of greasy and treacherous Jews. Alas!

FAIL BETTER: Failure may be a bitter pill but it doesn't define you, it just leads you to the next success. Take my time in America, for example, when my series *Frannie's Turn* didn't take off. People had said, 'You're going to be so rich you won't know what to do with yourself!' But when it failed, I was philosophical: 'Well, I tried it, and a television comedy series wasn't necessarily what I wanted.' Failure didn't knock me off my course. If I'd been a different kind of actress, it could have been a moment of great tragedy. But it wasn't.

Acting is a field of work in which one is failing repeatedly. Dear friends bolster my ego constantly; 'You've done so well,' they chorus, smiling. But inside, I never feel that. In America, they're afraid of two Fs – Fat and Failure. Perhaps because of my experience with the first, I'm less bothered by the second. In my book, success is making people happy. And failure is not accepting that there is always room for improvement. I love to think that I might create something unexpected even now.

FAMILY TREES: Genealogy must be about the living just as much as the dead. That's why a family tree is such a comforting thing. It's not just a list of names, but a plunging into a world that still continues – a group of funny, imperfect, often annoying but also loving and loveable people connected to me. When I look at my tree, I know I am part of an enormous linked chain of 15,000 souls – and growing! With that big a tribe, you can never be lonely. (See also **GENEALOGY**.)

FANDOM: I love having fans but they can become frightening when I realise that they want more from me than I can give – when they want to touch me and engage in conversation when I'm desperate to go to the loo, thrusting things to be signed in front of me and lurching forward to grab a kiss. That's where my walking sticks come in handy. I'm very short, but if I want to keep physical contact to a minimum, I can be my own bodyguard. 'GET BACK, YOU MIGHT GIVE ME COVID!' I shout, and they recoil. A particular dislike when I'm trapped in a wheelchair is when people swoop in and take me from behind without warning. But mostly my fans are sweet – either very young or very old, a delightful mixture across age and class. If not suffocated and swamped, I am ever delighted to meet those who like what I do. But if I'm clearly on the way to a loo – hang fire till I emerge!

FARTING: My firm belief is that it's always better to let a fart have its way, rather than try and sit on it. It never goes away. It cannot be that I'm the only person in the world who farts, who issues prior warnings of farts, who mentions farts they remember and who comforts those with uncontrollable wind. I'm happy to say I fart, Miriam is Windy City, but farting is no crime and as long as I don't shit myself, I count the world a sweet place to inhabit (if not always sweet-smelling).

FAT: Life, if you're fat, is a minefield – you have to pick your way through it, otherwise you blow up.

FELLATIO: Words are funny things. Fellatio could be the name of a road, but sucking off could only be sucking off.

FOOTLIGHTS: The Footlights were Cambridge's famous launchpad to an acting career. When I was there, a woman could not be a member: girls attended only as guests. So when I was asked to audition for a show called *Double Take* in 1962, I was delighted, if apprehensive. Mummy was overjoyed. She promptly phoned the *Oxford Mail* and gave an interview to them about my brilliance. This did not go down well with the rest of the cast, who included most of the founding members of *Monty Python* and *The Goodies*!

I was the only girl in the show. I couldn't sing or dance, I wasn't beautiful, but I knew I could be funny. The trouble was, they didn't really want 'the girl' to be funny. If you think about it, the *Monty Python* programmes didn't feature funny women, only the occasional dolly bird. And I certainly wasn't that. These chaps wanted to sleep with women, not compete with them. I was neither decorative nor bedworthy, and they found me unbearable. Cambridge was always a competitive place; in Footlights, it became toxic. During the entire run of *Double Take*, they treated me as if I were invisible. I was sent to Coventry. I would go on to do my bits, and then stepped off stage to silence and cold stares.

I'd never met studied cruelty like that before and it made me very unhappy. I used to go back to Newnham, and my loving friends on the top floor of Old Hall would sit me down in front of the gas fire, dry my tears, ply me with hot chocolate and explain that it was only to be expected from a group of emotionally stunted, minor-public-schoolboys. They may have tried to send me to Coventry, but I didn't have to go. So when I was deliberately left off the list for the cast party at the end of the show, I went to the head of the ADC and demanded the formal invitation I had earned – and I went.

In truth, my dislike of that largely male world of comedy has never left me. All the perpetrators went into Light Entertainment and I went into drama, so, thankfully, our paths seldom crossed. I admire the *Monty Python* creation and I think they were men of genius, but they were not (and did not become) gentlemen.

FORTRESSES: As I grew up, I often wondered, 'Why don't Mummy and Daddy have friends?' Because my parents didn't. Once the front door was shut, it was just us. Mummy had lots of acquaintances. She was sociable and hospitable, open and generous, but she didn't have proper conversations with people about her inner life. She called the three of us her 'fortress family'. We became her defence against the dangers of engaging with the outside world. In my case, my fortress has always been my friends.

FREE SPEECH: Sometimes openness can be destructive and pointless, but these days people often invoke 'honesty' or 'freedom of speech' in the most unnecessary situations. I've always had a foul mouth, and I'm sure I've been an outspoken old lady since I was a little girl, but I'm a firm believer that kindness rather than fear should moderate the truth. You should never be afraid to speak your mind but you should always be afraid of hurting someone.

FRICTION: Dame Sybil Thorndike was married to actor and director Lewis Casson for sixty-one years till his death in 1969. Once asked if divorce had ever been a possibility, she said, 'Divorce? Never. But murder, often!... If you are very healthy, highly developed people, naturally you have other attractions sometimes. Don't think you can go through life without thinking someone else is rather wonderful. I think the whole of marriage really in a way depends on friendship and being able to discuss things with each other, and not having any inhibitions about "I mustn't talk about this or it will make a friction". I think friction's fun.'

FRIGHTENER: It was Terry Donovan who introduced me to Slim in 1973, when Terry's building firm took on the renovation of my Clapham home. He was the foreman and came to check over the house and quote for the job. He was a gorgeous 'bit of rough', muscled, tattooed, totally confident in his masculinity. In earlier days, I'd have sucked him off like a shot. I sussed that he was an ex-con. I asked Terry later and he said: 'Oh, yeah! GBH a couple of times.' I filed that info away for later use.

And it happened a while later that one advertising firm owed me several thousand pounds for voice-overs. I phoned Slim and asked whether he would come round to see this advertising chap with me and encourage him to cough up – without actually touching him, of course!

He immediately said, 'Yeah, that's meat and drink to me. That's easy.'

So, flanked by Slim, I marched into the man's Soho office.

'Hello, Adrian,' I said.

'Oh, Miriam, how lovely to see you.'

'Well, Adrian, I don't know if it's that lovely to see *you*. I'm a bit pissed off because you haven't paid me yet.'

'Don't worry, I'll send you a cheque, Miriam. I'm sorry it's taken so long, sometimes these things get a bit delayed,' he said. 'I'll do it, honestly. I'll send you a cheque, it'll be coming soon.'

'Do you know what, Adrian? It's going to come even sooner than that. It's actually going to come now, right now,' I said, rather masterfully.

'I can't do it absolutely right now because …' He stopped.

'Oh yes, you can. Do you know how I know you can? Because Slim here …' I turned to Slim, standing silent and *powerful* beside me, and continued: 'Slim wants you to give it to me *now*, don't you, Slim?'

'Oh yeah,' said Slim, and stepped nearer to Adrian's desk. 'If you owe somebody money, you *have* to pay it, don't ya?' he said, softly but menacingly.

It had an instant effect. Slim was obviously not someone to mess with, and my debtor was visibly rattled.

'Oh … right, yes of course. OK, then,' he said, nervously. I got my money.

It was lovely knowing Slim in any case, but that was the only time I had to call upon him to put the screws on. He didn't do anything – he just stood there and was the Frightener – and that was quite enough.

FROCKS: There is a subtle difference between a frock and a dress. Mine are 'frocks'. They've all been made for me by various wardrobe mistresses on every film and play I've ever done. I look like a throwback to the 1950s, but they're comfy and suit me, and they ALL have pockets.

'FRUMMERS' are pious and observant people. My paternal grandparents were frummers – Mummy used to call them 'meshugannah frummers'. That kind of excessive religiosity troubled my parents, who were the generation of Jews who wanted to be ENGLISH – whereas once, in Jewish circles, the more observant you were, the closer to the Almighty. Now that religion has become embarrassing and irrelevant, I'm fascinated by frummers, and indeed I am a member of my local Chabad synagogue. My other shuls have closed and I really like the rabbi and his family. The problem is they have several beloved children, who all come to shul and pray loudly and it's not for me. I want my synagogue to be like Business Class on a flight: both child- and noise-free.

FUCK: When I hear Kenneth Tynan credited as being the first person to swear on television in 1965, I am irritated, because actually it was me – in the first series of *University Challenge* two years earlier. I have spent the last sixty years blocking out the expressions of frozen horror on the faces of my beloved Newnham College team of Susan Lee, Liz Hodgkin and the late Jinty Muir (the unspoken 'Oh Miriam!' far too clearly forming in all their minds) as a 'FUCK' burst out of my mouth.

The whole studio took in such a shocked deep breath that the willowy form of our bespectacled quizmaster, a very young Bamber Gascoigne, shook in the backdraught. He told me many years later that he had never forgotten the moment and he certainly rattled out the next question at double speed. I was duly bleeped out of the broadcast and thankfully the recordings are now lost. If only all my many other excursions into the profane had suffered a similar fate. (See also **TODAY**.)

'FUCKING HELL! THIS IS A FUCKING NIGHTMARE!': Swimming has always been my only exercise. I was in China filming with Wayne Sleep and we were told we were going to have a morning in a lovely big swimming pool in Chengdu. So, imagine clambering into a pool ready for a refreshing swim, only to find the water is stone cold and goes no higher than your ankles. Then you see the wave machine has been started. Giant waves are rumbling and rolling towards you: there's nowhere to escape. My gentle shriek emerged as more of a full-throated navvy-like bellow: 'THIS IS A FUCKING NIGHTMARE, FUCKING HELL!' A clip of my cry of mingled fear and rage was sent to TikTok, and became a meme that people have used almost a million times now as shorthand for when things have gone seriously wrong. I am still asked almost daily to shout it on my Cameos. Now, that *is* a fucking nightmare!

FUNERAL: When you're eighty-four, it's not morbid to reflect on your funeral plans, it's sensible. But I *was* taken aback yesterday when Heather, my partner of fifty-eight years, suddenly said in the kitchen, 'What do you want to do about your funeral?' She, the younger by two years, obviously expects me to go first.

When I pondered, I found it really hard to make a final, FINAL decision. How Jewish do I want it to be? Buried? Cremated? Scattered? Where held? What denomination of Judaism? I've decided to write my own eulogy, maybe record it myself, which will evoke both scorn, laughter and, I hope, tears. Is my funeral a three-line whip for close friends, or a gathering of all mates who could be bothered? Naturally, I'd want a full house and there *must* be a party – I'll set money aside for that. I'm getting sad already; I'm not ready to die. I want to live, I want some MORE.

GAGGING: My frequent fellatio has had one irritating long-term effect: visits to the dentist are often clouded by violent gag reflexes. My Australian dentists in Broken Hill (Cox – father and son) dealt with this issue superbly. They were somewhat surprised when I explained that it was a long time since I'd had two Cox in my mouth.

GAMP, SAIREY: Mrs Gamp is the drunken midwife from *Martin Chuzzlewit*. As well as delivering babies, a Victorian midwife laid out corpses, so Dickens described her as having 'a face for all occasions' because when the knock came at the door, she never knew what she would be needed for.

> I'm coming. Is it Mrs Perkins? What, Mr Whilks! Don't say it's you, Mr Whilks, and that poor creetur Mrs Whilks with not even a pincushion ready. Don't say it's you, Mr Whilks! And so the gentleman's dead, sir! Ah! The more's the pity. But it's what we must all come to. It's as certain as being born, except that we can't make our calculations as exact. Ah! Poor dear!
>
> Ah dear! When Gamp was summoned to his long home, and I see him a-lying in the hospital with a penny-piece on each eye, and his wooden leg under his left arm, I thought I should have fainted away. But I bore up. If it wasn't for the nerve a little sip of liquor gives me, I never could go through with what I sometimes has to do.

GAY: I love being gay. I wouldn't want to be straight for anything. There are those who resent the use of the word, which they think should be reserved for 'happy'. Tough shit folks: it's here to stay.

GENEALOGY: Genealogy allows us to be detectives in history. I have no family, no children, no husband, no parents, no brothers and sisters. Genealogy offers me the family I never had. I strongly recommend it. Piece of advice: write on the backs of the photos, in those boxes you find in the attic. That way, people can remain immortal.

GERUNDS: I'm still thrilled by the gerund. Let me explain that. When you say, 'I was surprised at him going to India,' it really should be: 'I was surprised at *his* going to India.' Do you see? It's somehow sweeter that way, slips more easily off the tongue. I'm always correcting people, and when I say, 'Don't forget the gerund takes the genitive!' they look blank and say, 'What? What?' And then I explain. And then they say, 'Oh, fuck off!'

GIN: My tipple of choice is a gin and tonic. (Four cubes of ice, cover them with the gin, add a slice of lemon. And then allow your guest to add the tonic to taste. I think it's rude to pour tonic on someone else's gin – it's like making them wear your knickers.) Mummy got me started on the gin at eleven. She said it would help with period pains. It did. For me, one glass does the trick, however. I become stunningly amusing; I release my inner Oscar Wilde. And then I announce to one and all, 'Grab these pearls while you can! Because in about twenty minutes, I will be asleep.' And I am.

GLUTTONY is eating to excess, which I have done all my life. My drug of choice is chopped liver, and lots of it. We Jews have a word for overeating – to *fress* – which, in my heart, I don't think is a vice but an essential pleasure. The word 'enough' is for me the sin – it's a killjoy, a party-pooper, an anti-life, finger-wagging blight on the world. Shut up and pass me the cheesecake!

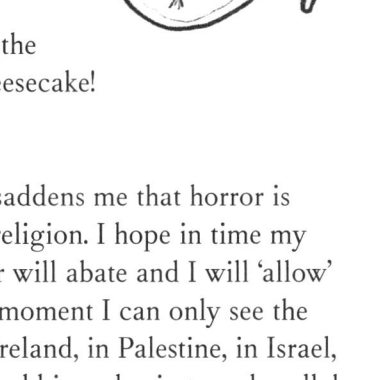

GOD: I see God as a giant fraud. It saddens me that horror is allowed to flourish in the name of religion. I hope in time my prejudices will lessen and my anger will abate and I will 'allow' religion in other people, but at the moment I can only see the harm it does: the deaths caused in Ireland, in Palestine, in Israel, in Iran, in India – everywhere that rabbis and priests and mullahs and imams and Scientologists spread lies and cause havoc in families and nations. God needs a smack.

GOOD ADVICE: Mummy always said, 'Go forward. Don't look at those on each side of you. Think about the road ahead. It's not about what other people are doing. What matters is what *you're* doing.'

GOOD GIRLS: In the words of Mae West, 'Good girls go to heaven but bad girls go everywhere.' Back in the day, a good girl didn't have intercourse, she sucked people off ... My prowess at oral sex was well known in Cambridge. I felt it was one of my best things – certainly the sexual activity I'd had the most experience of performing. It didn't matter to me whose penis was in my mouth, it was all grist to the mill; I knew I was giving pleasure, which was what delighted me.

GOSSIP: Gossip, as long as it's not malicious, is fun. But (tell it not in Gath), malicious gossip is even more fun!

GRAVE MATTERS: I'm a life member of Highgate Cemetery. It's not that I want to be buried there but I want the cemetery to be preserved. The Victorians 'did' death so well. Jewish people don't bring flowers when we visit a grave; we bring a stone. Flowers die, like people; stones don't. When I visited my parents at Wolvercote Cemetery in Oxford I only had one stone, so I nicked one from a nearby grave. I knew Wilfred. I didn't think he'd mind if I took one (which his family later confirmed). I only took a little one. I hope Daddy wasn't offended that his was only a little stone whereas Mummy's was big. But that was how it was – he was little and she was big. Death itself is just the end of things. But graves matter.

GROIN-TWITCH: The undeniable internal vulvic alert that you desire someone carnally.

GROWING UP: The truth is, I don't think I ever really did. Do we *have* to?

GROYNES: It gave me quite a turn when visiting Bexhill-on-Sea to learn that they call their wooden sea-breaks 'groynes'. Why? It's worrying, but then I should have guessed – it's a Tory stronghold and they're all arseholes.

GUESTS: Lady Whiteadder knew how to treat them.

> **Lady Whiteadder:** Edmund, I trust you have invited no other guests?
> **Blackadder:** Certainly not.
> **Lady Whiteadder:** Good. For where there are other guests, there are people to fornicate with.

GUIDES: From the Brownies ('Here we come, the sprightly Sprites, brave and gentle like the knights') I briefly graduated to the Girl Guides. I enjoyed knots, but a bowline on a bight and a reef were as far as I got. The embarrassment of roll call where my jutting breasts forced Miss Walkinshaw, the chief Guide, into a reluctant dance of two steps back and one sideways was the final straw. I left after two weeks.

HAIRBRUSH: The Californian lady professor whispered into my ear in a deep voice: 'The repertoire of love is wide.' When I didn't say anything, she enquired, 'Have you ever experienced pain in the course of love?' I said, 'No!' because, of course, I hadn't. Indeed, if anybody had tried to hurt me (never mind the 'repertoire of love'), I'd have biffed them from here to Doncaster. She then waxed lyrical about how magical and fantastic it was. I was anxious to please.

'Do you want me to hit you?' I ventured. 'Yes,' she answered: she would like me to hit her – with a hairbrush. I got out of bed, went to the dressing table and picked one up. 'This one?' I asked. It was a good-quality brush, a Mason Pearson as I remember, smooth black on one side, the bristles on the other. 'Yeah, why not?' Her eyes sparkled. 'I want you to *hurt* me.' I went back to the bed, somewhat anxiously. She turned over and exposed her buttocks. I raised the hairbrush high, bristles facing out and gave her bottom a tepid smack, rather lacking in lesbian flagellation technique.

I'm still an innocent in such advanced areas of pleasure and, while writing this, thought I should bone up on this area of inadequacy, though seldom now called upon to exercise such a craft. Google to the rescue. If I'd only known then, there's an informative website – *A Beginner's Guide to Impact Play* – which covers exactly what I'd needed. I read on ... 'A subculture known as Christian domestic discipline (CDD) promotes spanking of wives by their husbands as a form of punishment; some describe CDD as a form of abuse and controlling behaviour, but others consider it a simple sexual fetish and an outlet for sadomasochistic desires.' Let's leave it there.

Back to The Brush. 'Harder, much harder,' my professor mumbled indistinctly, her head in the pillows. 'Right,' I thought.

'Here goes –' and lifting the hairbrush above my head, brought it down with all my strength on her rear end. THWACK!

'*Not that hard!*' she screamed. Well, I didn't know, did I? I'd never make a good dominatrix.

HANDBAG: You might expect that I would echo Dame Edith Evans's famous handbag line as Lady Bracknell, but no actress can ever escape her shadow. Let me instead share with you the moment in July 2023 when *Vogue* magazine asked me to reveal the contents of my handbag on camera. It was brave of me, as a lady's handbag contains her Weapons of Mass Reconstruction. I think my tools may have surprised the crew. My snack of choice is a raw white onion, which I had to admit had already been chewed. It's my equivalent of a peppermint, with the advantage of keeping folk at arm's length in these Covid-infused times when Breath can be Death. Next: a spare clean pair of capacious navy-blue knickers is essential. Then my disabled status – I have spinal stenosis – is doubly confirmed by the treasured Blue Badge (which is what people want to steal, not my car, darling eighteen-year-old Fanny Fiesta) and the universal lavatory key which prevents agonising waits in motorway service stations while the staff member dawdles to open the disabled loo. But most of all, *Vogue* were particularly keen to know what beauty items I carry. That's easy. A lipstick; a small pot of Nivea to relieve dryness in whatever area you wish; and a pair of tweezers – *de rigueur* for every woman over thirty-five. And here's the proof if you want to see it: **https://www.youtube.com/watch?v=vy_v2BSst2M**

HANDJOB: If you looked in the Index for this, I know exactly what kind of person you are! But believe me, a handjob can be just the ticket in certain circumstances. I've given many over the years, but one in particular sticks out (as it were) in my memory. It was November 1970 and Patricia Gallimore (yes, Pat of *The Archers*) and I were travelling back to London from the island of Gozo after a short but delightful holiday. She had boarded the ferry with all our luggage, I was returning the hired car. It took longer than expected, and as I pelted down the ramp to join her on the ferry, I was horrified to see it slowly move away from me and start its journey to Valletta. Pat was on deck, saw it all and shrieked, 'Meet me at the hotel!' What to do now?

I walked round the tiny harbour and found a group of fishermen chatting in their rowing boats. 'Who will take me to Valletta?' A vigorous old chap in a denim boiler suit called up to me. 'You come with me, Miss. I take you.' Gratefully, I jumped down and he settled me in the seat at one end of his boat. He picked up the oars and we were off. It was a calm sea, a sunny day and he was smiling and friendly. We started to talk. He pointed out a nearby island. 'I take you there, Miss – we make love.' 'Er, no, I can't. You see, my friend is on that ferry and we're flying back to London today, I have to be back.' 'But is beautiful there, no people, we make love.' I noticed the button fly of his boiler suit was popping with activity. I was stuck in the middle of the ocean, alone, with a sexed-up septuagenarian – what was a girl to do? I wasted no time. I moved over to his seat where the rudder was. He tore at his flies and out popped a jutting purple member. I took the rudder in one hand, the member in the other, and steered us both to harbour. Luckily, it didn't take long and the seawater cleaned my relieving hand quite well. I offered to pay when we got to Valletta, but with a surprising sense of chivalry, he said, 'No charge, Miss.' I rushed to meet Pat. I explained how I had got there so quickly.

'What do you mean, you "tossed him off"? You pushed him overboard?'

'Noooo, Pat, I gave him a *handjob*.'

Pat was a nicely brought-up young lady – we are still the closest of friends. I phoned her just now to check the details. We agreed it was unlikely to happen again. 'Yes,' she said. 'Some ships have sailed!'

HARMONY HOUSE: This was another of Mummy's watchwords. 'I *must* have Harmony House!' I think what she really meant by it was that she brooked no disagreement, and tough shit if you wanted to stand in her way. She didn't believe in democracy.

HAVISHAM, MISS:

> In an arm-chair, with an elbow resting on the table and her head leaning on that hand, sat the strangest lady I have ever seen, or shall ever see.
> She was dressed in rich materials – satins, and lace, and silks – all of white. Her shoes were white. And she had a long white veil, and bridal flowers in her hair, but her hair was white. She had not quite finished dressing, for she had but one shoe on; the other was on the table near her hand.

I saw that everything within my view which ought to be white, had been white long ago, and had lost its lustre, and was faded and yellow. I saw that the dress had been put upon the rounded figure of a young woman, and that the figure upon which it now hung loose had shrunk to skin and bone.

'Who is it?'

'Pip, ma'am.'

'Pip?'

'Mr Pumblechook's boy, ma'am. Come – to play.'

'Come nearer; let me look at you. Come close.'

It was when I stood before her, avoiding her eyes, that I took note of the surrounding objects in detail, and saw that her watch had stopped at twenty minutes to nine, and that a clock in the room had stopped at twenty minutes to nine.

'Look at me. You are not afraid of a woman who has never seen the sun since you were born? Do you know what I touch here?'

'Yes, ma'am.'

'What do I touch?'

'Your heart.'

'Broken!'

Miss Havisham is one of my favourite Dickens characters.

HEREDITY: Mummy was the rock in my life. It was not that I didn't love my father, but he was quiet, and she was not. In some senses, they were incompatible. They came from very different strands of Jewish life. Mummy was the most vivid person I have ever known. She was an overflowing, ebullient, seemingly confident and, if I'm honest (and I must be), slightly vulgar person, while my father was totally buttoned up, very Presbyterian and hemmed in by all the orthodoxy of Judaism to which his family subscribed. My mother was more of a free spirit: accomplished and brave and fearless. While undeniably much more like my mother, I remain a strange mixture of them both to this day.

HERPES: What's the difference between love and herpes? Herpes is forever.

HOLIDAYS: Every summer holiday Daddy would drive us from Oxford through the Blackwall Tunnel, stop for fish and chips in Lewisham, and on to Percy Avenue, in Kingsgate in Kent. The local celebrity was Jack Warner, who played the eponymous Dixon of Dock Green, an old-fashioned benevolent copper, a world away from today's tarnished Metropolitan Police Force. But when I look back on my childhood, the sun was always shining. We spent whole days on the beaches of Botany Bay, Joss Bay, Broadstairs, Ramsgate and Margate. We did exactly what all the holidaymakers did – ate ice cream at Morelli's, went to Dreamland and gambled on the slot machines (only a penny then), watched the Punch and Judy shows and rode the donkeys. And Mummy made me take part in the end-of-the-pier talent competition; she was confident I'd win and I usually did. 'Martha' by Walter de la Mare always went down well:

'Once … Once upon a time …'
  Over and over again,
Martha would tell us her stories,
  In the hazel glen.

Hers were those clear gray eyes
  You watch, and the story seems
Told by their beautifulness
  Tranquil as dreams.

She'd sit with her two slim hands
  Clasped round her bended knees;
While we on our elbows lolled,
  And stared at ease.

Her voice and her narrow chin,
  Her grave small lovely head,
Seemed half the meaning
  Of the words she said.

'Once … Once upon a time …'
  Like a dream you dream in the night,
Fairies and gnomes stole out
  In the leaf-green light.

And her beauty far away
  Would fade, as her voice ran on,
Till hazel and summer sun
  And all were gone: –

All fordone and forgot;
  And like clouds in the height of the sky,
Our hearts stood still in the hush
  Of an age gone by.

HOLLYWOOD: Los Angeles is a strange mix of the exotic and the naff. It's not a city: it's a collection of neurotic neighbourhoods. But it does give you the opportunity of reinvention. They say you can be whatever you want to be there; I embraced that freedom wholeheartedly, but I had no intention of adopting any of the Californian lifestyles or fads: I don't believe in all their New Age nonsense. I might have dyed my hair once or twice for parts when I was in LA, but I never had any plastic surgery or tooth-whitening. I tried to steer a course between the Yiddisher Momma and the Venice Beach Girl – between Shelley Winters and Jane Fonda. I would say, on the whole, Shelley Winters won.

HOME: Neither Heather or I ever plan to retire, but I hope that perhaps we might be able to live in one town, in one place together. The highest joy I know is to be in the same room, either talking or silent, reading or watching a film, and looking upon her dear face and being grateful she's in my life, that I chose my partner so well and that we made a life together.

It may be that we will only actually finally get to live together properly when we're both in an old people's home. I always had the idea that we would build our own and gather all our friends there, and that's what I'd still like to do. There would be a library and a garden and memories shared. And animals. And a swimming pool, with easy steps down into the water.

HORSERADISH: I have never feared Authority – dictatorial and bossy myself, I have always answered back. I felt I was the equal of anyone: headmistress or factory foreman. I once had a holiday job in Frank Cooper's marmalade factory on Botley Road, where I was often cheeky to the foreman. The punishment for insubordination was being sent to the horseradish-sauce section. I spent a lot of time in horseradish. It certainly made your eyes water.

HOUSEWORK: Mummy did her housework in the nude. This was probably influenced by her membership of the League of Health and Beauty, a somewhat fascist ladies' exercise class which resembled the Luftwaffe in bulky knickers. Mummy was certainly one of very few Jewish ladies in it. She was too fat to stand on a chair to dust the lampshades; I'm grateful for that. But her ballet training stood her in good stead for our upright Hoover. Our various au pairs were initially shocked but bravely took it and her in their stride. Marie-Carmen, a well-brought-up *mademoiselle* from northern France, tried to explain: 'Your mother. I liked her but she was a little … how shall I say … different.' And she blushed. I knew exactly what she meant.

ICE-BREAKING: During the long months of the first lockdown, holed up on my own in Clapham, what I missed most was people. I longed for human contact – so much so, that I used to sit on my front steps and call out to those walking past. I would ask my neighbours where they were going and strike up conversations of surprising intimacy with complete strangers. If it were a couple, I asked if they were lovers or just friends and that often led to further tasty revelations. But my favourite targets were dog owners, old people and the disabled – all people who couldn't move fast enough to get away. As a recent cripple, I was always partial to mobility-scooter stories.

But what is strange is that the distancing Covid demanded has remained with me. I don't want to get close to people, I've stopped hugging strangers – I'm happy for front-gate chats and revelations. But closer encounters of any kind still feel unappealing.

ICE CREAM: I love ice cream. My fave flavour is coffee and my fave London supplier is Nardulli's on Clapham Common – and I think it's true, Italians do make the best ice cream and always have. Mummy used to talk about the 'hokey-pokey' made by Italian ice-cream sellers on bicycles, and her eyes went misty just recalling the flavour. I defined it on *This Morning* as what tongues are for. I do admit to other uses, but for the most part it's true.

ICED BUNS: Tim Walker smiled. 'Would you do a nude shot?' he asked. The *Vogue* shoot had been going very enjoyably until then. I froze. I did ask myself, 'What would Mummy think?' And then I thought, 'Oh, fuck it. OK, let's do it.' I stripped to my knickers

– and, apart from a pearl necklace, I was totally naked from the waist up. I was still nervous.

'Act. Imagine you're playing a model. I want you to be Barbara Goalen,' Tim said, picking up his camera, and we were off.

Then two glass cake-stands of iced buns appeared. I had noticed some young men carting boxes and boxes of cream cakes and Victoria sponges through the house earlier – I thought they were to feed the crew. But no; each adorned with a central glacé cherry, these large buns were my new costume.

IDENTITY: Memory is identity and that's the tragedy of dementia. When you lose your memory, you lose yourself. The description of a person can be a cluster of adjectives and/or pronouns. There's no end of adjectives – and pronouns – available which can be used to call up a person, a whole human being. 'Lesbian' need not be a definitive noun. It should be just another adjective. I'm lesbian, I'm short, I'm fat, I'm Jewish, I'm Dickensian. Many *different* things. At the time of writing, Trump (you know who I mean) has just decreed there's only two sexes. Poor fellow. I expect he felt challenged by the multiplicity of initials; well – it is confusing but you can't play God with front bottoms. They matter.

IMPOSTER: My mother taught me how to spot an imposter, a liar, a phoney. She had a sixth sense for untruth. Now I'm equally adept – and proud of my quick annihilations of spam merchants.

When they phone, always at lunchtime, with a scheme to make money and ask for me by name, I simply say sadly: 'Oh, she died about three weeks ago.' They ring off sharpish!

INCONTINENCE: My body is taking its revenge. And my bladder is weak, or is it my sphincter? All I know is that it is a pissing nuisance. Every time I go out now, I have to check where the nearest loo is, as when I need it I have about ten seconds to get there. I always carry a spare pair of knickers. I am obliged to drink a lot of water because of my kidneys – oh the Organ Recital is so BORING! I just wish I'd done Pelvic Floor Exercises when I could. (See also **OLD AGE (OR THE ORGAN RECITAL)**.)

INFANTA OF CASTILE: In 1982, I leapt at the chance to play the mad Spanish Infanta, along with Jim Broadbent as Don Speekingleesh, my interpreter, in the first series of *Blackadder*. In my episode, 'The Queen of Spain's Beard', the king (Brian Blessed) decides to cement an alliance between England and Spain, by marrying his second son Edmund Blackadder to the Spanish Infanta. Edmund is excited at the prospect until, that is, my entrance as the Infanta – a short, plump, sexually rampant princess with a monobrow and a hint of hirsutism around the upper lip and chin. I often describe myself as an 'overactress', but I must say my appearance in *Blackadder* as the irrepressibly lascivious Spanish Infanta is one of the performances in my life which I can truly say is *not* understated. I delivered all my lines in voluble and babbling Spanish (which I don't speak), all the while licking my lips and making eyes at a terrified Rowan Atkinson, with his skinny little insect legs in black hose and that awful Henry V bowl-cut hairdo.

> Infanta: *Oh, amor mio! amor mio!* [*Kisses Edmund.*]
> Don Speekingleesh [*translating*]: My love, my love.
> [*The kiss lasts for several seconds, bringing Edmund to his feet; finally he is able to push away.*]
> Infanta: *Oh! Me gustan tus labios!*
> Don Speekingleesh: Your lips I like.
> [*Edmund gingerly feels his lips, as though they may have been sucked off.*]
> Infanta: *Es el resto de tu cuerpo lo que me interesa!*
> Don Speekingleesh: It is the rest of your body I wish to find out more about.
> [*Infanta licks her lips, Edmund covers his face, then peeks through a couple of fingers for a moment before covering it again.*]

INTELLIGENCE: I once described myself as 'extremely unintelligent', but I no longer think it's sensible for me to say that I'm *extremely* unintelligent. I can't do IQ tests and I'm completely innumerate, for example, but I can remember telephone numbers, so perhaps a more accurate self-assessment would be that I am a little bit thick.

INTERNET: In my admittedly limited experience, the three most prominent areas on the internet seem to be: pornography, cats and genealogy. I've dabbled in all three. Cats win every time.

INTIMACY: One of the ways that acting works is that you need to expose yourself. You must immediately be open to the person with whom you're working. In ordinary life you try *not* to reveal yourself: you cover up. And that is considered good manners because you don't want to go *bleurgh* over everybody. Most normal people can't handle that, but in the theatre, you expect to be intimate immediately. Part of the pleasure of friendship is to be confident in exposing yourself. I remember Susan Andrews (my Newnham friend) exploding, 'Give me some *space*, Miriam.' At the time I was puzzled. I thought, 'What is she talking about? Why is she so cross? Am I standing too close to her?' I just didn't understand. I do now.

INTIMACY COORDINATOR: A new job has appeared in films: the 'intimacy coordinator'. Actors now need advice as to how to conduct the sex scenes and where best to stow those naughty bits that might change shape and get in the way. Unlike Kate Winslet and Helen Mirren, who are expected to appear nude in every part, I, on the other hand, am positively begged to keep my clothes on. But I think it's helpful to have a no-nonsense approach to below-the-waist acting, and answer the question, 'Whose climax *is* it, anyway?'

INTUITION: When acting, I tend to let my instinct guide me and hope for the best. When I read a text, I use the bricks of my own personality to build a character. It's the text that gives you the mortar, the other elements of what you're creating and what you have in your mind's eye. When I get a play script, I want to see if the character has changed at all during the course of the piece.

Is there an emotional arc to the character? Or, if not, does she move in any way from beginning to end? If there is no movement, I have to try to put it there, because it's boring to know everything about a character from the minute they step onto the stage. The actor or actress must surprise the audience in order to engage them and to entertain them. That's what I look for in the writing. But the surprise must be organic, from within. Imposing it won't work.

IRL (IN REAL LIFE): Wandering through the backstreets of Giglio in the autumn of 1970, looking into an open doorway, Heather suddenly burst out laughing. Therein framed was a scene where a young man, dressed only in what she described as 'psychedelic budgie smugglers', was enthusiastically treading grapes. The old and the new Italy joined together. Heather stayed outside but, much to her embarrassment, I burst in and started talking to him. Within five minutes we were all firm friends. I still rush towards unexpected encounters.

ISRAEL: I well remember the creation of the State of Israel in 1948. I was nine and I knew it was important, but my father was not happy. 'Mark my words,' he said. 'This will bring trouble for the Jewish people.' Unlike nearly everyone I knew in our small Oxford Jewish community, he was not a Zionist. I went there first on a ZIM cruise ship from Marseilles to Haifa when I was seventeen, to work on a **KIBBUTZ**. I was afraid to fly, so took the more expensive, slower option of a boat and stepped into the steaming hot, busy harbour and saw the poster with Herzl's words on the wall: *If You Will It, It Is No Dream.*

As I read that, I recognised the desperate longing for a home, to be safe, at last. It made me weep then – and I'm still weeping. I've made many visits there to relatives and friends, and on one visit, I was taken by the United Nations over to Gaza. Poverty, dust, crowds of children. They threw stones, they instantly knew I was Jewish. I couldn't blame them – I was the enemy. Since then, I have often visited the West Bank and made friends there. Israel is making a terrible mistake in its treatment of the Palestinians. They will *never* relinquish their land. I can only pray for a ceasefire and for a shared state.
It's unpleasant to be vilified by those I love who have disagreed with me, publicly and viciously. But I am sure that I am right; we Jews have become the abusers. My heart is heavy – it means Hitler has won.

JAM: Memory's a strange thing. **MARMALADE** makes me think of teenage rebellion but jam always leaves me melancholic. One of the most poignant memories I have of my mother, Ruth, was on one of my visits from London. After her devastating second stroke, we were shopping in the supermarket Fine Fare in North Oxford; I'd made a list of what was needed and there was something Mummy seemed agitated about, something she wanted me to buy and was anxiously looking for on every shelf. In 1968, she had lost the use of her speech and could only say two phrases: 'Pouf I want' and 'I can't afford a carriage'. Her frustration and despair growing, she kept stabbing the air and the shelves she could reach. Try as I might, I couldn't work out what this object was. I decided to park Mummy's wheelchair at the far end of the store and finish the shopping on my own. Suddenly I heard a tremendous scream. 'JAAAMM!' Mummy shrieked at the top of her voice. 'JAM, JAM, JAAAAM!!' Shop assistants came running from everywhere, panicked by the fierceness of the cries. Other customers gathered around, mystified, and I rushed to Mummy. I found her pointing at a shelf of Tiptree jams, laughing with joy and crying with rage all at the same time. I cuddled her and calmed her and realised how lucky we are to be able to communicate our needs. Jam will forever be linked to this moment of profound sadness and sudden unlikely celebration. Shopping has never been the same since.

JAMES AND THE GIANT PEACH: In Henry Selick and Tim Burton's Disney production of Roald Dahl's *James and the Giant Peach* (1996), Joanna Lumley and I played the orphan James's sadistic and tyrannical aunts. Wonderful Joanna was Spiker, the beautiful, thin, nasty one with a vicious tongue, and I was Sponge, the fat, vain one, who delights in admiring herself in the mirror. The film combined stop-frame animation and live action scenes. It was the first time Henry had worked with live actors not puppets. He kept asking us to perform impossible tasks, like running backwards uphill. On one memorable occasion he wanted me to fall downstairs, and then as I lay there dazed, a live tarantula would walk across my face. I insisted on a stunt double to do the fall, and I spoke to the spider wrangler beforehand: 'Is he sedated?' I asked. 'Oh, yes,' said the wrangler. 'He's a naturally friendly guy, but his poison sac is intact, or he wouldn't move.' I said to Henry: 'Darling, I'll give you one shot at this.' I lay on my back at the bottom of the stairs, the tarantula was carefully placed on my forehead, and the cameras rolled. A tarantula has eight walking legs and two pedipalps that are used for touching and moving prey. Eight little, cold feet walked slowly across my face. I didn't know about the pedipalps, I just knew about the feet. I didn't move or tremble, I tried to think friendly thoughts. Henry got his one shot.

Another stunt Joanna and I were persuaded into was being winched sixty feet up, strapped back-to-back with ropes, standing on a tiny round manhole cover, being spun centrifugally in the air and drenched with water from fire hoses directed straight at us. I thought, 'If I have to die in a film, being strapped to Lumley is not a bad way to go!' Our stunt captain was called Rocky (natch!). A sweet guy, he knew we were scared and said, 'The minute you want to come down, just shout "Rocky" and I'll have you brought down right away.' I think we lasted fifteen seconds, then we both screamed 'ROCKEEE!' at the tops of our voices. And down we came. Never again.

JANE EYRE: I can remember reading *Jane Eyre* and nearly exploding with pleasure at the line, 'Reader, I married him.' Sorry, that was a bit of a spoiler, but nevertheless, I do urge you to read it. Those Brontë girls knew how to inhabit and convey emotion, and considering it was written in 1847, the book is bristling with sexual longing. An American thesis exists with the title: 'Jane Eyre, the Invisible Bisexual'. But I wouldn't worry your pretty little head about that.

JEALOUSY: Some people are great fun to be with, but suddenly they can get up and bite you. Such people are 'frenemies' – they cannot resist the cruel dart. A true friend is someone who delights in and brings out the best in you, and when you're in their presence, you feel enriched and happy. A frenemy revels in your weak points and says spiky and negative things, leaving you dissatisfied with yourself. Nobody needs that kind of person in their life; Mummy always said, 'Stay away from jealous people.' And I do.

JESUS: I've got a soft spot for Jesus, or Joshua Ben Joseph as he would have been called then. Not as the Son of GOD – I can't accept that – but as a good egg, who made kindness and honesty a commandment. I never got around to reading Book Two but I bless his sweetness. He always sounded like a nice young carpenter; a caring, decent bloke and a firm socialist to boot. Though packed with churches, the Oxford I grew up in would have sent him packing without a thought.

JEW, BEING A: I can't answer the question, 'What is a Jew?' And sometimes I wonder why I have to. I just know I am one: a non-believing Jew. I'm militantly secular – religion has caused so much horror in the world – but I believe in tradition. I'm proud of my roots: they nourish me. I want to honour the past, honour my parents, my ancestors and all those who died, and so I follow many of the Jewish practices. I always fast on the Day of Atonement (Yom Kippur), maintain the dietary restrictions during Passover (no leavened bread etc.), and have never eaten bacon, shellfish of any kind, rabbit, ham or pork, in any guise. I may not believe in God, but I'm fascinated by the pull of Judaism and its culture – the food, the jokes, the vitality, the suffering, the guilt and the history – it's all part of who I am and what I've inherited. The fact of my being Jewish informs the whole of my life.

I acknowledge there is a contradiction at the heart of my attitude. I reject any religion which teaches discrimination and divides people; I deplore the contempt that so often Jews have for Gentiles. You didn't know that, did you? And yet, I LOVE being Jewish. It's one of the first things I say when I introduce myself. I declaim it from the roof tops. When *Spamalot* was in preview, I remember I went along with the rest of the *Wicked* cast. There's a bit in the show where King Arthur (Tim Curry) asks, 'Are there any Jews here?' – naturally, I bellowed back at the top of my lungs, 'YEEEEESSSSSS!' After a slightly surprised pause, Tim replied, 'Jolly good!'

When I was invited to be on *Desert Island Discs*, one of the pieces of music I chose was the Kol Nidrei, because the fine ethics of the Jewish religion inform my life. I relish the chopped liver, the matzah balls, I am defiantly proud of my Jewishness and its rich traditions. I may not observe all of them but I insist on their being recognised. Each year, on 27 January, I remember the six million, including my own relatives, who were murdered in the Holocaust. Its lesson is never to forget. I never can. I never will.

JEWDAR: 'Are you Jewish?' is the question I most often ask strangers, though only if my 'Jewdar' has been alerted – by someone's looks, their voice or, most often, their surname. Sometimes people bristle, but I am just trying to connect.

So how do I spot the others of my kind? Often, it's someone's name that gives it away. Before 1787, Jews didn't have last names, but Emperor Joseph II decreed that all Jews in the Habsburg Empire must adopt fixed hereditary surnames. And the names were assigned by administrative clerks, often using the names of materials (gold, silver, diamond, cotton); or trees (Birnbaum: pear tree; Kirschbaum: cherry tree); or, as in my family, physical characteristics of the man (Gelbard: yellow beard; Grosskopf: big head). People took their names from rivers or towns near their home (Posner: from Posen; Danziger: from Danzig). But sometimes you just look at someone and you can tell their Jewish origin – like me.

JOHN, AUGUSTUS: I wanted to meet Augustus John after seeing him on TV in *Face to Face*, so I wrote and offered to model for him at no cost. I was seventeen. Mummy and Daddy meekly drove me hours across England to his Fordingbridge studio in the New Forest and left me alone with the artist notorious for his sexual appetite and many illegitimate children – and it came to pass that I took all my clothes off and he stroked his great beard and nodded appreciatively. 'Your skin takes the light,' he growled in his old-man voice. And I purred with pleasure. I wasn't embarrassed (which surprised me) and I wasn't scared. I felt quite safe. And once he'd finished drawing, he taught me to play shove ha'penny until Mummy and Daddy arrived to take me home.

JOHNSON, BORIS AND STANLEY: I was in a reality TV show with Stanley Johnson and stuck in Britain under his son as prime minister and sadly the libel lawyers won't allow me to say why I now believe very strongly that the rotten apple doesn't fall far from the diseased tree.

JOKE ONE: (I only know two jokes, and this is the first.) There were two old Jewish men: Morrie and Abie. Every week, they would meet up, regular as clockwork. So, this week, Abie totters into Morrie's house, sits down; Morrie's wife brings him a lemon tea with two lumps of sugar, the same for Abie. And Morrie says, 'Abie, have I got something to tell you.'

'So tell me!' said Abie.

Morrie says, 'Well, you know how me and the wife always like to go to a nice restaurant? Something a little different, you know, not every night, but from time to time? And this week, oy! Did we strike lucky.'

'So tell me,' Abie said.

'Well, we go into this beautiful restaurant. Pleasant lighting, lovely ambience, not too noisy, comfy seats. The waiter comes up, he gives me the menu. Oy! Such a menu! It was delicious. A bit of chopped liver on the side with rye. Then a little chicken soup with matzah balls, of course. Then something a little different: I had spinach. I never have spinach, but they say spinach is good for you, so I had spinach. Then there was the beef brisket, and then we had the carrots, roast potatoes, peas, a little side of baked aubergine ...' And he goes through the whole meal with Abie, listing every side dish and the entire contents of the dessert trolley.

Abie says, 'Nice, nice, very nice.'

And Morrie said, 'I was so happy, I was satisfied, and you know what, it was reasonable – not too expensive. The price was right, the food was good. Amazing! Where do you find such a thing?'

Abie says, 'Exactly, Morrie. Where *do* you find such a thing? What's the name of the restaurant? You sit here telling me all about the food you ate. What's the name of the restaurant? Don't keep it to yourself like that! Tell me.'

Morrie says, 'Of course I'll tell you! What do you think? We're friends for fifty years and I'm not gonna tell you the name of the restaurant?'

There was a pause and he said, 'The name of the restaurant is ... Oh my God. *What is it?* What's the name? Wait a second. Aha! I got it. There's a flower, comes in all colours, beautiful perfume, but you gotta be careful, it's got thorns on it. What d'ye call it, that flower?'

'Oh,' says Abie. 'You mean, like a rose?'

'That's it,' says Morrie. 'Rose. ROSE! *What's the name of the restaurant?*'

JOKE TWO is about a typical New York Jewish grandmother. Every week, Grandma Ruthie takes her grandson Sheldon to the beach at Coney Island. They sit on the beach, have a picnic and talk to each other – a precious moment in both of their lives. So, this day, they're at the beach. It's a glorious clear sunny day, not a cloud in the brilliant blue sky: no rocks, beautiful golden sand and sparkling green sea. She's sitting on a blanket with the picnic she's lovingly prepared. And little Sheldon is playing close to the waves. She's always looking to make sure he's safe, to see the chubby little figure toddling across the sands and paddling in the shallow sea. And when she looks up, she sees that whereas it *had* been a lovely sunny day, now it was turning blustery. And ominous dark clouds were forming rather quickly. The sea was getting a little wild and the wind was coming up. A storm was building. And then in the distance, and suddenly not in the distance, but frighteningly close, a huge wave comes rolling and rumbling towards the shore ... and snatches the little boy, her precious darling Sheldon, and hurls him out to sea.

Grandma Ruthie is desperate. She runs from one end of the beach to the other, crying, 'My grandson! My grandson! Sheldon! Sheldon! Help me, help me! Help me, please! He's drowning in the sea!' But Sheldon had vanished into the violent churning depths. And then she falls on her knees and calls out to God. She raises her hands to the Almighty and she beseeches, 'Please, Lord. Don't take him away from me. All my life I keep all the Commandments. I keep a kosher house, I light the candles every Shabbos, I fast Yom Kippur. I do everything you ask of me, God. Now, down on my knees I am begging you, PLEASE, bring back Sheldon to me!'

And amazingly, the sea calms, the wind dies down, the clouds seem to disappear. The sun comes out and in the distance another wave comes forward, gentler, gentler. And slowly but surely, she sees little Sheldon, her beloved grandson, being borne on the crest of a wave in towards the shore. And finally, he is gently placed down at her feet. Grandma Ruthie falls on her knees again, raises her hands to the skies, and calls out to the Almighty, 'HE HAD A HAT!!!'

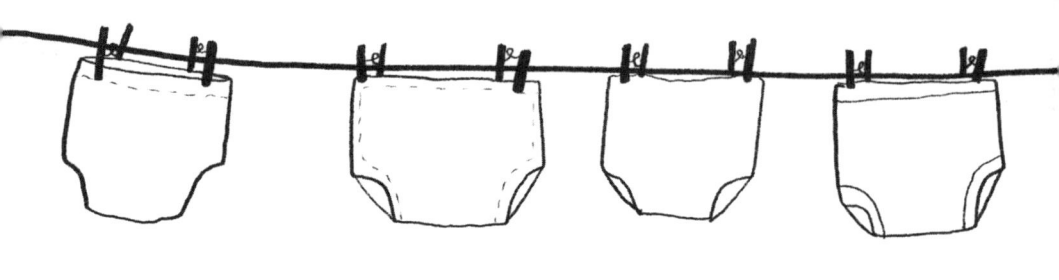

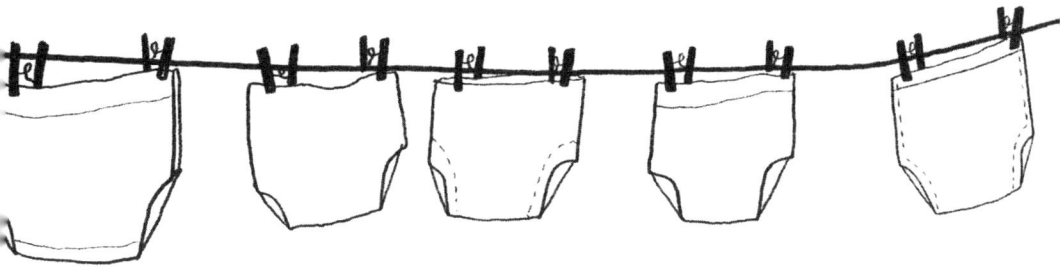

KIBBUTZ: In the 1960s it was just the thing for a nice middle-class Jewish child to do – to go and work on a kibbutz in Israel. Kibbutzim are small communities rooted in socialist ideals for communal living, with political life associated with the left wing and peace solutions. My family were not Zionists, although the little blue tin collection box for Israel was always on the hall table. It was all my decision. I knew I ought to learn Hebrew and I'd met Naomi Assenheim, a wonderful Israeli girl and was inspired by her. She suggested Kibbutz Urim in the Negev. And so, one long school holiday, I went. On arrival, I was told my job was to wash dishes in the kitchens for five hundred kibbutzniks. This was *not* the job I'd wanted; I hate housework and deeply resented being stuck indoors. After a couple of days, I requested a transfer to the orange groves. I could see myself plucking bright oranges from green trees in the sunlight, surrounded by happy Pioneers singing rousing worksongs. Au contraire. It was appallingly hot; I sweated all day and I didn't like my fellow pickers at all. Their aggressive attitude to the neighbouring Arabs was unappealing. I didn't argue back at the time, but it made me feel uncomfortable. I stuck it out for a few weeks and then left. I never returned. Looking at Urim now, I realise it was six miles from the border with Gaza, and destined to be in the eye of the storm, which is still there.

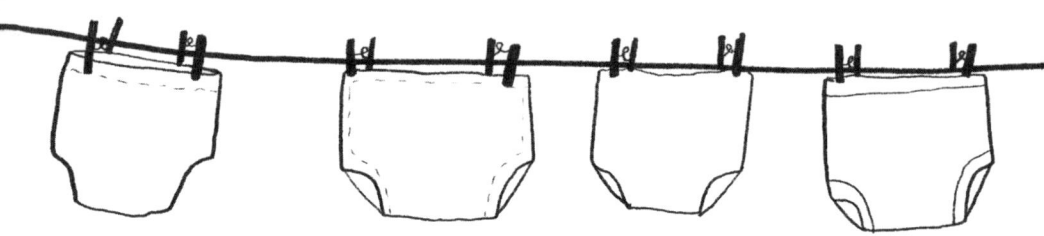

KIKE: This isn't a happy word; it's a vile one shouted at Jews to show hatred and scorn. Millwall fans sometimes yell it at Tottenham fans during a football match, and recently it's come back into fashion. Now anti-Zionism and antisemitism have been conflated into one thing, I fear it will be shouted at me. It saddens me to resume acquaintance with a slur from the last century I had thought was dead and gone. We seem to be living in the 1930s again – and we know what that fine mess turned into.

KINDNESS: The surge of cruelty and stupidity that surrounds us has shocked me, and I've come to realise that the quality I most value is kindness.

KING, THE: I met King Charles when he was the Prince of Wales. He had listened to my audio-recording of *Oliver Twist* and generously hand-wrote a letter of praise and appreciation, delivered by a royal car to my Clapham home. I couldn't believe it: I kept thinking, 'If only my parents were alive!' And since then, I have been invited to Sandringham, to Buckingham Palace, to Clarence House, and we have talked about Charles Dickens in all those places. I like and respect him, although I am politically a socialist. He cares about the planet, the country, all the people of the United Kingdom. He is human and honest, fundamentally

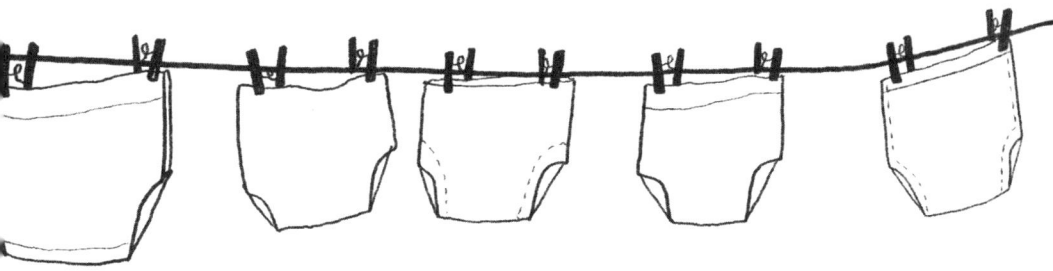

serious but with a glorious sense of humour. He could have been an actor; I've seen him work and I would employ him like a shot. I am not his friend – to claim that would be an impertinence. But I know enough to believe in his decency and kindness, and when I read some of the ghastly stuff newspapers write, I rush to defend him wherever I can. I value his worth. We are lucky to have such a king. I wish him health and strength and a long and happy life with his beloved queen, who is totally delicious. I've been swimming with her and I KNOW.

KISSING: I kissed Bob Monkhouse once. Forgive the non sequitur. It was in a BBC television play, *Enter Solly Gold*, by Bernard Kops. I was playing a small part but Bob Monkhouse was Solly Gold. In one scene, he had to kiss me. It was the best kiss I think I've ever had: slow, searching, not slurpy. I thought, 'If I was straight, I would go for Bob.'

KNICKERS: Ken Dodd and I used to say 'knickers' to each other when we needed cheering up. I love the word, because it makes people giggle like schoolchildren. Only the British would count that as a naughty word, though.

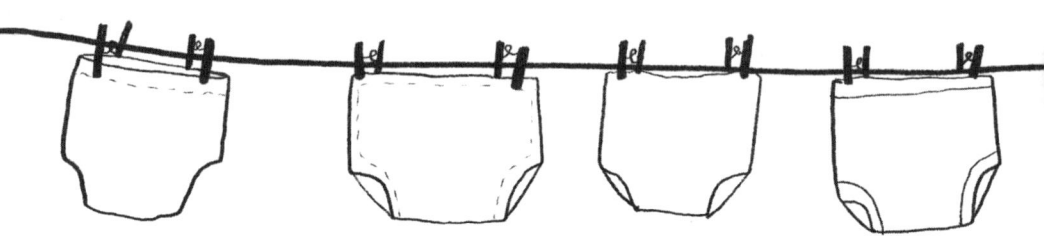

KNITWEAR: My coverall of choice, whatever the weather, comes from the beautiful island of Aran. I detest the word 'sweater', which not only has American connotations but is odoriferously redolent of exercise. My Aran cardigans are chunky, hand-knitted and very warm. Their patterns recall butch fishermen, a look I have long admired, and I wear my two favourites interchangeably, one dark burgundy, another in algae green.

KOALAS AND KANGAROOS: I am soppy about animals. There are two glorious marsupials I've become familiar with since I started to be an Australian. Both are symbols of the country but both are treated in a cavalier manner that is very Australian. Koalas are dying out because of a chlamydia infection, not the one transmitted sexually which humans get but another variety which is lethal to the little darlings. They're the mascot of Australia and yet fighting to avoid extinction. Wildfires and destruction of their habitats make life perilous; but should you pick one up and cuddle it, you will become their slave for life. All those marsupials are moreish; koalas are more my size; kangaroos are definitely not.

In our Aussie country retreat, we see them at dusk, standing on their back legs watching us driving up the track to the house. They're often in family groups, the father and mother grey and quite tall, looking at us looking at them – then they

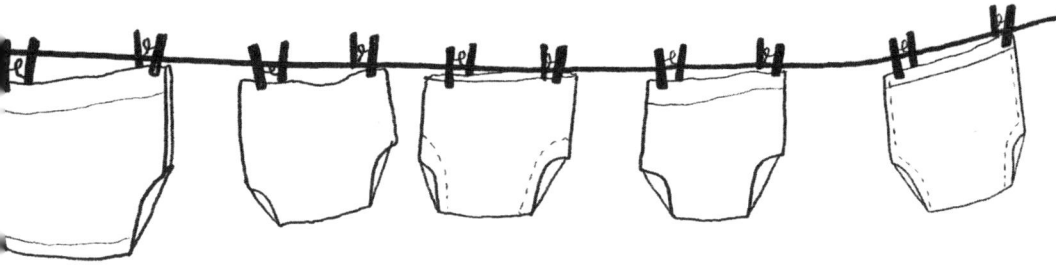

all bound across the hill, the two younger roos following, covering the ground very fast in great bounces, merging quickly into the surrounding landscape – their fur is an accurate camouflage. Seeing wild animals in their natural habitat is always a thrill, a present to make you smile and feel grateful. Thousands are killed on the roads every year and sometimes offered for supper. I once ate some, having been told it was 'just' lamb. It was undeniably tasty but I was cross to have been fooled.

K

LADY, BEING A: Mummy and Daddy told me firmly, 'You must behave like a lady,' which meant you mustn't sleep with people before you're married – which I took to heart and, rather like President Clinton, I interpreted it in my own way.

LANDLORDS are probably as unpopular as estate agents in the public mind, but I learned from the best. My mother, searching for a way to supplement my single-handed GP father's income when they arrived in Oxford after their East Ham house was bombed in 1940, realised that the one thing always needed in Oxford was student accommodation. She started out small and ended small, with four houses – the last one at 122 Woodstock Road, which I wish she'd never sold. But her houses attracted the cream of Oxford high flyers. We had Lord Jacob Rothschild, Francis Hope, Paul Betjeman, Tariq Ali (who still owes £100), the late former MP Robert Maclennan, Hugh Fearnley-Whittingstall, Rachael Pakenham, Ken Loach and Ferdy Mount. She regarded her relationship with her tenants as much more *in loco parentis* than any other landlord I know. And she never overcharged. She taught me to fix things immediately if they went wrong. She also taught me to make friends with plumbers and electricians, to pay tradesmen 50 per cent up front, the rest on completion, and to go to auction sales for furniture. People who buy new are nuts!

My favourite landlord was Leonard Sagar, a lampshade maker. I loved living in 108 Gloucester Terrace: the entire house was inhabited by gays (except for Leonard and Sybil, who lived in the basement). This was never acknowledged. The closest we got was when I fell out of bed with a massive thud, in the middle of the night after a particularly active sexual romp, Mr Sagar shouted upstairs, 'Are you all right, Miriam?' It must have quite alarmed them as they slept below me. I reassured them, and our lives went on.

LAUGH: Would I do anything for a laugh? You know, I think I would.

LAUGHTER: When I go to a funeral – and I've been to a hell of a lot – I want to celebrate, not just to mourn. I want to experience the black humour of true memories, finding joy in those shared stories of the dead with all the chums, and laughing together. That's what I love most. I think laughter is better than God.

LAZINESS: Even as a foetus, I was lazy. I had to be cut out of my mother, as she often reminded me. And I have never exerted myself since – skiving off from games, curling up with a book or a woman whenever action was expected. I enjoy work, but activity, moving the body – never. I even ask people to pass me the chocolate biscuits.

LEAVIS (AND BEING A LEAVISITE): Frank and Queenie Leavis were my teachers in the English Faculty at Cambridge. For me they were the personification of intellectual vigour, rigour and excellence, but they were loathed by most of their colleagues. It was mutual. Dr Leavis didn't hesitate to ridicule and show his scorn for his colleagues. His particular bêtes noires were Brigadier Tom Henn, Master of St Catharine's College, and

E. M. Forster. We giggled at the acidulous remarks that dripped from his quiet voice. There was a curious, slightly dying fall to his sentences – the opposite of theatrical, but in its very opposition to theatricality, it was *unbelievably* dramatic. He fascinated me.

Frank Leavis was never made a Professor at Cambridge; in fact, he was never elected to a higher status than Reader at the university, because there was such combined opposition to him. He had to fight every step of the way. But to his students, he was, and is, a hero. It was when I was listening to Dr Leavis that I felt I was drinking in knowledge, that I was with the best people, that I had fulfilled my mother's dream. Dr Leavis was, above all, a superb teacher. He opened the delights of English literature to me and thereby enriched my life. At his final lecture, the hall was packed, people standing in the aisles when all the seats had been filled. His slight figure, gown billowing, came out. He gave the lecture, and then paused. 'I've come to the end,' he said, with his characteristic dying cadence. 'And this is the end.' Not a dry eye in the house.

LEFT-WING, BECOMING: I came from a middle-class Jewish background, always Tory-voting, supporting capital punishment and rejoicing in the British Empire. And then at Oxford High School, when I became friends with Liz Hodgkin I was changed into somebody with a heart. I've never looked back.

LESBIANS: Don't get me wrong, I love being a lesbian, I'm all in favour of cunt and women loving each other, but honestly, it is an ADJECTIVE, not a NOUN, and I insist on telling my dykey chums to make sure they belong in the world and not just the gay world. Don't let those who want to divide people push us into a corner. Let's join up the dots; don't demonise the Other, or we become as bad as they are. We're lucky we're gay women; we can be who we want to be. And if you haven't tried it yet, don't wait too long. I recommend keeping your nails short and direct eye-to-eye glances. It works for me.

L

LIFT ETIQUETTE: Whilst a keen believer in letting it go, it is good manners *not* to fart in a lift – and I would only do that if I know everyone in it. The problem comes when the doors open and the lift takes in more people and the fart is still there. Here is where etiquette comes into play – I always own up. I claim the fart as mine; I would never expect another to bear the shame of a fart to which they didn't contribute. I have noticed others are not so scrupulous, pointedly staring at someone else, mutely accusing them of the something for which they should own responsibility. This is a test of morality and many are found wanting.

'LIKE': My pet aversion, 'like', is an excuse for the cessation of thought. A lazy habit that has escalated irritatingly through our language. You might say, 'It was, like, Tuesday' – there is NOTHING like Tuesday. I have been known to explode into violence when I hear the word several times in a sentence. Once on a train from Richmond to Clapham, I burst into someone else's perfectly pleasant conversation: 'Like … like … like … like …'

'Do you know how many times you've said the word? SEVENTY-TWO!' I shrieked at the surprised couple. The man was most offended: 'I'm not watching any of your films again.'

LIMELIGHT, DON'T HOG THE: I have worked with actors who deliberately keep moving while someone else is talking, start knitting in the middle of someone else's speech or noisily open a letter. If it's someone else's moment, you *have* to pass the baton.

LINES: The dread of forgetting one's lines, I think, is the basis of all anxiety in the theatre, and so it has been for me. As I get older, it feels ever more perilous – even thinking about it now makes me feel nervous. In 1979, I was in Snoo Wilson's *Flaming Bodies* at the ICA. The play started with an eight-page monologue and I just couldn't remember it. My panic built up during rehearsals and by the afternoon of our first night, I was in such a state of terror that I told Julie Walters that I couldn't do it, and I wasn't going to go on. She was shocked that I was even entertaining the idea. The show must ALWAYS go on. 'Don't worry, Miriam. You'll remember it. It'll be all right on the night. You'll be fine.' 'No, I fucking won't,' I wailed. 'It's hopeless!' And I ran out of the ICA and jumped into a passing black cab. Julie, in hot pursuit, jumped straight in after me. We then spent the next few hours driving around London as the taxi meter clicked up relentlessly and she desperately tried to talk me round. Poor Julie! But I was adamant: I'd had days to panic about it and I knew I couldn't remember those eight pages. On we drove – I wasn't even distracted by the sight of the meter devouring my meagre salary – but eventually we stopped and paid the taxi driver off. He was happy, at least, and then we went for a cup of tea. I didn't do the performance that first night – but I did it on the second and it was fine – good even! Alas, I never worked with Julie again but I will never forget her kindness to me.

LIVING IN A FRIDGE: I have played many bizarre roles in my long career, but perhaps the oddest was in a film called *Ed and His Dead Mother* where Steve Buscemi played the eponymous Ed, and his dead mother was … *me*. When I am brought back from the dead, I take up residence in the refrigerator so as not to go off. It was only a half-size fridge and rather cramped, so perhaps it's hardly surprising that before long my character is swearing like a trooper, jumping over nine-foot fences, chasing dogs and cats, wielding a carving knife and chainsaw on a ride-on mower on a killing spree. Rather than his dream of having his mother back, poor Steve ends up having to kill me, but it's most reluctantly. He remains to this day the only person who has ever fed me cockroaches, which he did with love and the utmost politeness.

LODGERS: Mummy was a landlord; you're only a landlady if you provide bed and breakfast. I would never do that, but for fifty years I have shared my house with younger people – occasionally a couple, often Australians, whose breezy, ironic friendliness delighted me. Now I have very English Emily and George, not together, sleeping next door to each other in my top bedrooms. The interview process to find my lodgers is stringent and searching. But I always say, 'You can ask me any question I ask you.' Sex and drugs are swiftly sorted (I provide neither) but quiet sex is encouraged as long as they KNOW the person. I won't allow pick-ups – not in Clapham!

George is thirty-two, Emily is thirty-one; they're taller than me (hard to be shorter) so they can reach things down for me. I live in the basement now to provide maximum separation but we all look after each other. They have their own front door and strict instructions to be mouse-like ascending the stairs. Every morning,

I telephone and one of them reports for Bra Duty. This tends to be George, who is quite adept. He also makes the most delicious coffee and walnut cakes. Emily is in charge of technology, fixes my TV viewing and knows all the *Doctor Who* luminaries. In return, they both come to *The Graham Norton Show* with me, and George even took part in my *Vogue* shoot. They're family now – better than children and far more interesting.

Emily is a TV development executive; she's just written a book about her distant relative, Grace Darling, the famous heroine of lighthouse rescue. The rescuing ability clearly runs in the family. George is an actor – he was in *The Mousetrap* when we met – and has since rigged up a recording studio in my old sitting room for audiobooks and commercials. They come to me for life advice. Our special relationship is currently being turned into a TV sitcom. Not a romcom. Don't get your hopes up!

LONDON: I came to London as a green girl after university. I loved it, was excited by the clamour, speed, variety and danger of the city. I slept on friends' floors and in rented flats; I lived peripatetically in Plaistow, in Earl's Court, in Lancaster Gate, in Paddington (Mummy called it Bayswater) for twelve years, and then finally bought a lovely five-bedroomed Victorian house in Clapham for £21,500 with a loan from my parents. Now I can't wait to leave. London was once the place an aspiring actor had to live – that's probably still true. But what *I* need has changed. I want peace and quiet, not wealthy party-giving neighbours with leaf blowers and firework parties. And London has changed into a place where only the rich can live. It's violent, crime-ridden and clogged with traffic. Even tottering along the pavement with my walker is fraught with peril, attempting to avoid electric bikes and scooters, discarded sofas and roadworks, never mind the thieves aiming for my mobile phone. Now I want to move to a small anonymous country town of innocence and casual beauty. Or to New Zealand.

LOOK AT ME: From birth I have wanted to connect with people. Mummy told me how I followed everyone with my gaze, even from the pram. And it worked! People were always stopping her in the street and asking to look at me, exclaiming, 'Oh, what a beautiful baby!' I was indeed ferociously gorgeous.

LOVE: Love isn't sex, but sex is always welcome of course. Love is being entirely comfortable with someone and enjoying their contributions between the ears as well as between the legs. I was a late starter in love and it was worth waiting for. I'm glad I didn't have to rely on the internet: Bumble, Tinder and Bender sound like an ambulance-chasing legal firm. The minute I saw Heather I knew she was the one. She didn't, but we've stayed together for fifty-eight years, largely I think because we have never lived together. Now we're ready to. Hope it works.

LYING: You can usually tell from people's eyes if they're lying. It's the eyes that give it away, the little darting, oblique glances, the frequent blinking. But conversely, if they don't turn away, if they stare unrelentingly, if they try to fix and hold your gaze to theirs, that can also be a sign of a lie.

MAKE THE MOST OF IT! Look at me. I may be old. I may be walking with sticks. I may rattle with pills. (Why are there so many pills to take when you get old?) But I'm still here and I'm still earning. What more do you want? Stop moaning and get on with it!

MANIKIN CIGARS: They are always asking for sex in adverts. Possibly my strangest advert, certainly the sexiest, was when I deepened my high girlish tones for Manikin Cigars. I was the darkly sultry voice of Carole Augustine, a beautiful young British model and actress (who had made a brief appearance in *Confessions of a Window Cleaner*). In the ad she stood beside a tropical waterfall, all in white, revealing a gorgeous tanned midriff and cleavage. While she was dipping a tobacco leaf in the water of a rock pool and stretching it lasciviously across her lips, I had to say, 'I come to show why Manikin flavour plenty enjoyable. I need water. See? Water make leaf stretch. Wrap cigar well. Mouth enjoy flavour. Yes? Manikin flavour special.'

I did a whole string of these ads – presumably all the different films shot on that one same trip to Antigua – with the lines: 'Manikin bring you best tobacco. Tobacco plant tall. Manikin wrapped only with tobacco picked from middle. Middle leaf best, make Manikin cigar special'; 'Manikin tobacco fermented ... Make cigar smooth and mellow, so Manikin flavour pleasing to man. Manikin flavour special.' All ending with the words 'Sheer enjoyment' sung to the familiar tune. It was one of the

most successful advertising campaigns of all time – look it up on YouTube – but now it feels like a relic from another age: cultural appropriation of the most aural kind.

MANNERS: Old and disabled people should be taken care of. When I get on a train and I need to sit down, I ask politely, 'Please, may I sit down?' Once on the Underground, I was feeling exhausted and my back was hurting badly. I saw a young man seated in front of me. When he didn't stand up to offer me his seat, I didn't wait or have an argument, I plonked myself on his lap! He was surprised, then really quite angry, but he got up pretty quickly. I consider he had the bad manners, not me.

I've noticed it's usually women who offer their seats. Men rarely bother; they pretend to be too engrossed in a newspaper to notice if someone needs to sit down. But good manners still matter. You should always be as polite, careful and caring to people as you possibly can be. But if people are nasty and cruel, then fuck it – they've got it coming.

MARCHES, GOING ON: When I was young, protesting was a holy duty and marches were the means of protesting. The one I should have gone on and didn't was the Aldermaston anti-nuclear march in 1959. Lots of lesbians, lots of passionate people; I just didn't have the guts. I did march for an end to apartheid, and the abolition of the death penalty; against Trident missiles; for the repeal of Clause 28 (in my lifetime any discussion of homosexuality in schools was considered its 'promotion') – and we were listened to. Today the climate of protest has changed; it's angrier, more violent and desperate. But those who attempt to control the rage and frustration seem moronic. Racism, anti-Black, antisemitism, anti-Muslim, climate-change wars – not a weekend goes by without a confrontational march. But I can't march any more, I can hardly walk. Age wins; but my need to stand up and be counted remains the same.

M

MARGOLYES: That's my name, but for some reason everyone always spells it Margoyles. I can't tell you how cross I get about that. Jenia Reissar, the revered casting director, told me to change it in 1964. I refused her advice; I'm not sorry I did. At least it's only two names, not Nyree Dawn Porter or Paul Thomas Anderson. I just tell people it ends with YES and rhymes with FLEAS. Got it now?

MARMALADE: I've always preferred orange marmalade to jam. And even more after my vacation job at Frank Cooper's marmalade factory, where I stirred the boiling vats of Seville oranges and had to wear a silly muslin hat, like all the other factory workers. But this is my favourite marmalade story. In 1973, I bought my Clapham house. It was in a bad state and while I got the money for the renovation, I installed five or six

friends in the bedrooms using all four floors, all happily paying £2 a week.

Every Friday, I would go and collect the rent in cash. In the basement flat next door were Mr and Mrs Smith, a couple who'd lived there since the war. One day, when I was collecting the rent, Mrs Smith was in the front garden. She called out, 'Mirian [she never could say 'Miriam'], I want to talk to you, come over here. Listen, this is a nice road. We've never had rubbish on this street, Mirian.'

'No. I'm well aware of that,' I replied.

'Well, those friends of yours ...' She paused for effect. 'The other day I was out doing the weeding, and I 'appened to look across into your big bay window up there. You'd never guess what I saw – it was them two in there [*pause*], stark naked [*pause*], eatin' marmalade. Well, we can't have that in *this* street. I mean, people in the nood? I don't want to see *nothing* like that again.'

I told my friends, 'Please don't eat marmalade naked in the front window, it really upset Mrs Smith.'

I don't know if it was straight out of the jar, but Mrs Smith must have had a very long look to know it was marmalade and not jam.

MARRIAGE, THE TEN COMMANDMENTS OF: Here are my ten tips on how to stay married:

1. A ROOM OF ONE'S OWN – Virginia Woolf suggested that every woman needs a room of her own. I heartily agree. But to my mind, *everyone* needs private space, to think, reflect, be oneself. It's creative separation.
2. TALK TO EACH OTHER (and listen to what the other says), ESPECIALLY DURING SEX.
3. SEX DOESN'T LAST, SO ENJOY IT WHILE YOU CAN – a good RADISH is better than bad sex.
4. RELISH THE DIFFERENCES BETWEEN YOU – don't try to make the other the same as you.
5. BE KIND. BE RESPECTFUL – words can bite and wound. Don't do it.
6. DON'T GAMBLE WITH YOUR HAPPINESS – just being married doesn't stop your noticing another possibility. But it's seldom worth it. Like giving into your desire for lemon meringue pie, a moment on the lips and then forever in the shit.
7. DON'T FUDGE, DON'T BE GLIB – this person knows you and still loves you.
8. IF YOU'RE NOT HAPPY, FACE IT – AND TALK ABOUT IT!

9. NEVER LET THE SUN SET ON A QUARREL – a true cliché.
10. MARRIAGE IS WORK IN PROGRESS – so adapt. Cuddles become more important than penetration.

MATHS was the opposite of sexy (despite all the possibilities offered by multiplication). I know at some point maths can become philosophy and there's an exciting branch called topology, but it never seemed worth the struggle. Miss Jackson (my humane maths teacher at Oxford High School) said, 'Miriam, you're dreadful at maths – there's no point in pretending – and frankly, I don't think arithmetic is worth doing either.' I knew it was hopeless and I dropped maths from my life from that moment. I can make money, I just can't count it.

MEANNESS: Daddy was mean, Mummy was generous. Actually, the whole Margolyes family had short arms and deep pockets. The Turiansky family, who married into the Margolyes family, are still scornful about their meanness. But this was partly because my grandfather, Philip Margolyes, was extremely poor when he arrived in Scotland in 1870. I'm a mixture of the two. I'll buy any amount of food when treating people at a restaurant but always announce at the beginning that I won't pay for drinks. On the other hand, I tip generously; but if the service is poor, I tell them. At home, I do serve large gin and tonics as an aperitif – but nothing else. If you want wine, BYO.

MEEP: Sometimes, you think Life has passed you by. And then – all of a sudden – it hasn't. Although I had attended various Harry Potter fan meets, when Sylvester McCoy told me about the joys of the *Doctor Who* conventions I had felt a strong pang of envy – despite never having been a Dr Whosie Floozie or even part of the vast audience through the years the Doctor had ruled the small screen. I had once come close when wonderful, lengthily bescarfed Tom Baker tried hard to get me on board as his time-travelling companion. But sadly the Powers That Be issued him a robot dog called K9 instead. And after that I assumed that *Doctor Who* and all the delights promised in that cornucopia of Invention had disappeared forever.

But then last year, out of the blue, a cunning little monster, sweet of face, innocent and winsome of expression, enticed me to be its wheedling voice: 'Please be my friend. Why won't you speak to the little Meep? Be my friend. Be my friend!'

White and furry, resembling a flat-faced overgrown kitten, the Meep is vile and rotten to the core. The arc of its character from Angel to Devil is skilfully written and in a North London voice studio, it came to life and flourished. It was the greatest fun to switch into horror, to astonish and confound my many

victims. And now I have entered the Halls of *Doctor Who*, joining the ranks of the sci-fi multitudes of Monsters and am entitled to attend the Conventions, and canoodle my way into the hearts and minds of the Willing Whoozers around the world. All I need is my psychedelic army. Initially I thought The Meep was a female monster, but now, I realise, it's beyond sex.

'I am the Beep of All the Meeps ... My chosen pronoun is the definite article. I am always The Meep.'

MEMORY: What we remember creates who we are. In my earliest memory, it is a sunny day, and I am in the front paved area of 159a Banbury Road, sitting in my pram, observing the passing traffic. It was a more innocent world then; children could be left to play in the front garden without being kidnapped. I was a pretty child, with big, dark eyes and a most winning smile. A brisk lady passing by, stopped and came up to me. She said, 'If you don't stop sucking your thumb, the bogeyman will come with his scissors and cut it off!' I remember feeling such scorn that this woman could tell me such nonsense, expect me to believe and succumb to her threats. I felt utter contempt for her, for the flagrant lie she told (bogeyman indeed!) and for her impudence in interrupting my pram reverie. She left me and continued her journey. But my utter rejection of her nonsense is with me still. I have resisted bullying my entire life, and I know it started then.

MEN: When you find a good one, it's a real treat. But most aren't quite formed; they've been spoilt by their mothers and expect to be looked after, deferred to and to run the show. I feel a bit sorry for them. How can you take Jacob Rees-Mogg seriously? Or indeed, at all? But sometimes, you have to fight back. I mustn't generalise, but really, most of them need a good smack. Women just are better. 'Nuff said.

METROPOLITAN MUSEUM: I stood at the Reception Desk at the Metropolitan Museum in New York.

> Receptionist: I'm sorry, ma'am, the Gertrude Stein portrait is not on display today, the gallery's closed for refurbishment.
> Me: What? Nonsense. You don't understand. I've come all the way from England to see this picture. I'm an actress. I'm just about to play the part of Gertrude Stein in London. I have to see it. Please call the curator!
> Receptionist: You want me to call the curator?
> Me: Yes, please.
> Receptionist: OK ma'am, just a second, please. – Hello, Mrs Cohen? There's a young lady at the Front Desk who wants to see the Gertrude Stein portrait. Yeah, I told her it's not on display, but she's an actress. She's kind of ... overexcited. Would you be able to come

out and talk with her? Thank you. – You're in luck! Mrs Cohen will be right out. She'll meet you by the totem pole.

Me: What totem pole?

Receptionist: Ma'am, *that* totem pole, right over there. It's thirty feet high. You can't miss it.

Me: Oh, sorry. Yes, I see it. Thank you.

I went and stood by the totem pole. In a few moments, Mrs Cohen came out. She gave me a long look and said, 'Good morning, I understand you want to see the Gertrude Stein portrait. Follow me.' I followed her through the museum from one end to the other, along corridors, through galleries. We came to an elevator. We got in and went down, down, down, all the way to the sub-basement, where they store the pictures not on display. And, again, we walked from one end of the room to the other.

We turned a corner, and there, leaning against the wall, was Picasso's Gertrude Stein, looking straight at me. The pose was one I was to adopt for the play: leaning forward, hands on her knees, with a thoughtful gaze – that's how the show opened. You could not escape the eyes; there was a kindness in them I hadn't expected. When Gertrude died in 1946, Alice B. Toklas phoned Picasso and invited him to come and say goodbye to the picture, the night before it was sent to the Metropolitan Museum, as Gertrude had stipulated in her will. He stood in front of his great masterpiece, painted forty years earlier, and saluted it.

MIGRANTS: When did they become migrants and not immigrants? We have hardened in our attitudes to people from somewhere else. We need to be kinder, more aware of the horrors people are fleeing from. Prejudice and nastiness (otherwise known as the Reform Party) are gathering forces. Hateful and wrong.

MIRIAM: My name, Miriam, means 'bitter', 'star of the sea' and 'longed-for-child', but the meanings were immaterial. Mummy named me after her favourite aunt, her mother's sister – a dark, pretty little woman, who died a widow in 1933.

MOBBED: I have to be honest; it's lovely being famous. The only time it has ever really become too much, I was in Vilnius, at a ballet matinee, enjoying the show. During the interval, I was jumped on by a screaming gaggle of mostly female, teenage Harry Potter fans. They completely surrounded me, shoving autograph books and flashing mobile phones in my face. They couldn't understand why I ran away! But I couldn't forget that the last time Jews were mobbed in Lithuania, they ended up dead. Then I got over myself, took a deep breath, smiled sweetly and signed some autographs. Scariest *Swan Lake* I ever attended.

MODERATION: Whose idea was that? No, my whole soul cries out in opposition – *Excess* is the key, not moderation. Moderation is skimpy, under-privileged, morose. It's the Puritan ethic which I scorn and fear. It's a party-pooping, life-denying ordinance, a finger-wagging locked larder door of a mindset. And yet ... and yet, it might cure fat, and diabetes, and I would be slender and even more magnificent. Dream on, MM: it just ain't happening. Alas and hoorah!

MONEY is one of life's essentials and there's no point pretending that it isn't. It matters how you earn money, what you do with it, and how you spend it. I was always brought up to have a healthy respect for money, and not to waste it. I like round figures. I *am* a round figure.

MORAL COMPASS: My principal gripe with the modern world is the lack of moral compass. No one cares about right or wrong: all they want is power and profit. When Trump promised to build hotel complexes along the Gazan seafront, no Western world leader expressed their horror or even disapproval. The deadly golden pager gifted to Trump by Netanyahu is another example of utter moral vacuity. What would their mothers say? Mine said: 'Do the right thing, Miriam!'

MUMMY: Without a doubt, the most important person in my life was my mother. Perhaps she still is. She died in 1974 when I was thirty-three, but she has never left my side.

Mummy was short and stout, with wavy grey-white hair, piercing blue eyes, a high forehead and a generous mouth. (She looked a lot like Gracie Fields, whom she admired greatly.) She stood very straight and was always telling me to do the same – shoulders back, head erect, no slouching.

She was the most intelligent yet untutored woman that I ever met. Mummy was always the soldier – the general of my army. She would never stand for anybody hurting me or subduing my thunder. In other circumstances, she could have been the head of a company or leading the government: but she came from a poor background and she was always conscious of that. Like Charles Dickens, she had sprung from the lower middle class. It's an uncomfortable situation: hampered by poverty and strongly aspirational, she observed keenly the class distinctions which exist in England. She wanted to speak well and meet 'the best people'. She was anxious always to separate herself from the 'common'. The odd thing was that she was endlessly generous to anyone poorer than herself. But she was squeezed in the trap of 'class' – and feared being at the bottom of the social scale. She was a passionate and determined social climber. Her dictum: 'It's not what you know, it's *who* you know that counts.'

Whatever talents I have come from my mother. Mummy really wanted to be an actress herself but of course nice Jewish girls

didn't do that then. But she never lost the ability to be dramatic in every way. She took centre-stage in our lives. She was the star. My mother did everything possible to give me confidence and make me feel special and talented. And when I hear pieces of music that she liked, I weep. I think it's true that the people you've loved in your life never leave you, because seeds of that love always remain, flowering somewhere.

M

N

NAPOLITANA, LA: The people in my Italian village, Montisi, give everyone a nickname. Mine was *la napolitana*, which I thought meant 'the whore', but is actually the 'Neapolitan lady' or 'the lady from Naples', which could carry all kinds of spicy connotations. I've since been assured it was inspired by my black hair, cheeky face, big dark eyes, dramatic manner, rather large breasts, and because I 'speak with my body'. The Montisani immediately sussed that I was one of the *stranieri furbi*: 'naughty foreigners'.

NAUGHTINESS: I was particularly naughty at school. The school day was brimming with opportunities for Miriam misbehaviour and I was almost always in trouble. On one frightful occasion, I noticed a child bending over in the corridor in front of me and, never able to resist temptation, I ran toward the proffered bottom and gave it a resounding THWACK! The figure straightened up with a snap and, to my horror, I saw it was not a child but Miss Maddron, the head of French. Miss Maddron was one of the special ones: though tiny and slim, she wielded immediate and powerful authority. The abject shock on my face was enough to clear me of any impertinence, and not a word was said as I fled up the corridor. On my last day at school, saying goodbye, Miss Maddron told me, 'You were naughty, Miriam, but you were never wicked.'

NEVER FORGET: When I was seven years old, my father's refugee patients would sometimes show me the numbers on their arms. 'What is that?' I asked them. I don't remember their answers; they said nothing that stays in my mind or hinted at horror. Inevitably, I learned about the camps. That knowledge fuelled my genealogical hobby, now an obsession. It has also coloured my feelings about the world that let it happen and is still letting it happen. It makes me sharper at spotting antisemitism. Thanks to Israel's continuing aggressions against the Palestinians, it is on the rise again throughout the world. It's now more crucial than ever to acknowledge what happened – avoiding the truth is so easy.

NEW FRIENDS: It is very important, the older you get, to keep making new friends. Firstly, the old ones will keep dying; secondly every friend refreshes the soul. Every new job yields at least one new friend – they don't have a choice, which is why my phone contains 11,739 people, everyone essential. I can't jettison people.

NEW ZEALAND: Despite my Jewish rellies who followed a well-worn path from Scotland to New Zealand, my knowledge of this small nation of just over 5 million people was superficial until my loyal documentary gurus in Sydney, Southern Pictures, offered me a glorious opportunity to travel around New Zealand, meet real people and learn about the islands. The unique and powerful landscapes of extreme variety overwhelmed me; hot springs, volcanoes, towering rock formations take your breath away. It is truly the most beautiful place I have ever seen.

I began to learn what it is like to be a Kiwi. Some of my experiences were decidedly outside my comfort zone: watching rugby (a game I loathe but it's the national sport) with 30,000 die-hard fans, and visiting Hobbiton – I met Tolkien in Oxford as a child: he would be as bemused as I am at these grown-ups living in a fantasy world. Yet I longed to go inside the neat little hobbit homes and sit in the hobbit scaled-down furniture, built as it seemed just for little me! I loved getting to grips with the *haka*, being taught how to do a *pūkana* (the Maori method of staring wildly: something I was strangely good at), and meeting the lawyer who fought and won the case to give the Whanganui River legally acknowledged personhood. Most New Zealanders exhibit a genuine reticence and old-fashioned good manners which reminds me of England sixty years ago – they're charming and guileless. And like the rest of the Covid-ridden world, I was delighted and impressed by Jacinda Ardern, their young prime minister at the time. Her compassionate reaction to events seemed utterly honest, unlike all the other lying world leaders. New Zealand has issues to sort out but it was impressive to see their fervent wish emerging to protect past achievements. Extremism is not admired; they deal with the inevitable inherited colonial history with good sense. And besides, who could fail to love a country whose national dish is pavlova?

NHS: I was seven years old when the NHS was created. My father was a GP with a small list of patients; he never earned a great deal, but he wasn't a doctor for the money. Although he was a Tory through and through, he strongly approved of the NHS. My father would hate what medicine has become; hard-pressed doctors aren't allowed to spend time on their patients, forced to keep to an unrealistic timetable and to rush you out of their surgery as quickly as possible. Thanks to years of Tory austerity, our Health Service is dying. We must fight for it to survive. Never forget its superb objective: free at the point of need.

NIPPLES: In puberty my breasts were urgent. My nipples were like bullets. I always had holes in the flimsy wool of my school jumper because they pushed through. I remember the Head of French, Miss Maddron, who was herself very short, had an uninterrupted view. As she was no taller than the smallest child, they were bang on her eye level. Her comment was crisp but kind: 'Oh Miriam, I think you'd better get your jersey mended.' It was a constant feature of my school life – two nipple-shaped holes forever requiring a stern darn. In those days, they were quite buoyant. Not any more: I do wear a bra but it's a Salvation Army job (**RAISING THE FALLEN**) rather than a genuine Lift and Separate.

NORTHERN IRELAND: There is an old joke in Northern Ireland about a tourist who gets lost in Belfast. Straying into a no-man's-land between Protestant and Catholic neighbourhoods, a balaclava-clad man grabs him and asks: 'Are you a Protestant or a Catholic?' The tourist stammers: 'I'm a Jew. I'm a Jew.' And the masked man says: 'That's all very well, but are you a Protestant Jew or a Catholic Jew?' Levity aside, I'd just like to point out that per head of population, the Northern Irish are the most generous donators to charity in the world.

'NORWEGIAN WOOD' is a Beatles song about a mysterious girl who turns up, sparks passion and then vanishes for ever. I experienced my very own Norwegian Wood in 1966 when I got picked up on the Central Line by a girl dressed in multicoloured trousers. It was the way she looked at me that started it off. Somehow or other, and I'm really not quite sure how, we ended up back at my flat, at that time very near to Lancaster Gate tube. We didn't sleep together; heavy petting would be the right term, but it was arousing. It was my turning point and after it, even when I went to synagogue, all I could think about was sex, and how much I wanted to have love affairs with other women. I had promised my parents I wouldn't, but some things are outside one's control. Turns out she was Norwegian; later, when Heather and I had met and I was telling her about it, she called her 'Norwegian Wood'. (It was only years later I had any idea what she was talking about as I avoided The Beatles and all pop music.) Rather appropriately, Mummy and Daddy went to Norway for their honeymoon!

NOSE-PICKING: It is true – I enjoy nose-picking more than any nice Jewish girl should. I don't know why there's a particular pleasure in nose-picking at traffic lights but there is. As the red STOP sign appears, the pleasure starts. I don't eat my bogies – that's a retch too far – but I love exploring each nostril thoroughly, then inspecting the result and finally flicking it out of the window. Fun to see the shock on other drivers' faces as I drive off. Small pleasures perhaps, but intense.

NUDITY: I envy those with lovely bodies, and if mine were lovely, I might give it a go, but I'm not my mother, I don't enjoy exposing myself any more and I think it's over-used.

And I definitely think blokes should keep their bits to themselves – there's so much *more* of the male pudenda than we offer, dangling about, positively *threatening* in their shorts. Ballet for a while was unwatchable for me; I was gasping at the bulging tights but I've got over them now and can enjoy the grace and power and the skill. I am glad people don't dance in the nude. Too much for this old lady.

OBE: In 2002, a thick, creamy-white envelope, embossed with the royal insignia, was delivered, announcing that I had been awarded an OBE for Services to Drama. A lot of people were quite surprised, none more so than me. Some people think that because of my political views, I shouldn't have accepted my OBE. Of course I shouldn't have. I know that; it goes against everything I believe in. But I most certainly wasn't going to turn it down.

When you get 'the nod', you're not supposed to tell anybody, and I didn't. But the only way I could keep it to myself was to go swimming; I swam on my back and whispered happily into the chlorine-scented air, 'I've got an OBE. I've got an OBE!' Against all the odds I had made it, I had been honoured by the Establishment.

As the queen was observing mourning for her mother who had just died, it was Prince Charles who performed the presentation at Buckingham Palace that day. And as he pinned on my gong, he said, 'Oh, I am so delighted to be able to give you this.' I was delighted too; I think perhaps he enjoys my enthusiasm more than his mother did: he has done more than anyone to make me a royalist. Aren't we lucky to have him as our Head of State and not the Orange Turd?

'OH MIRIAM!': As the result of my uncontrollable **NAUGHTINESS**, I spent a great deal of time outside our headmistress Miss Stack's door in disgrace, waiting to be summoned into her office. She would sigh as I strode in again: 'Oh Miriam! What is it this time?'

The exclamation 'Oh Miriam!' has been such a constant refrain in my life, said in all kinds of tones – laughs and surprised gasps sadly rather outweighing the orgasmic sighs (though there have been plenty of those too) – that I chose it as the title of my second book. *

OLD AGE (OR THE ORGAN RECITAL): Whenever I have Reunions (nowadays it's never just Unions) with my surviving contemporaries, behind the gossip, the constant theme is the miseries and indignities of old age. We compare ailments, we list our frailties, we closely observe the number of wrinkles, or walking aids, or memory lapses of our friends while we repeatedly say, 'Well, it's better than the alternative.' But is it? My TAVI (cow's aortic valve insertion through the groin) has saved me for a few extra years. But one titanium knee is all I'm having. It's fifteen years old – hope it stays the course. Should I have the misfortune to become doubly incontinent, I shall bow out.

---

*Available in all good bookshops

Switzerland will beckon, or the Netherlands. I shan't bother with operations. So I urge all women to do their Pelvic Floor Exercises in good time. And fellers – get that PSA test. Don't say I didn't warn you.

OLIVER TWIST: I discovered Charles **DICKENS** when I was eleven, through the pages of *Oliver Twist*. I have loved the world Dickens demands you enter ever since. With hindsight, it's possible that his delight in the criminal world, his compassion for the poor and his sense of mischief (the Artful Dodger) meshed with my own emerging personality.

After *Oliver Twist*, I went through all fifteen novels – Dickens created over 2,000 characters. And there is a lot more – 14,000 letters (no, I haven't read all of them), as well as novellas, journalism, speeches. Words poured out of him. More than any other writer I can think of, Dickens distilled his life into his work. Though a genius, I can't help thinking that he was a complete bastard, or I should say rather that he was an *incomplete* bastard, because he wasn't *totally* shitty. But when he turned against you, he had a cruelty and viciousness that was almost unhinged. All this runs through his books.

Throughout his life he felt underprivileged. He overcompensated by being a dandy. With his big, flouncy neckties and the flourishes of his hands, when he went to America some people thought this foppish figure terribly vulgar. His signature was absurdly pretentious; rather like that of Queen

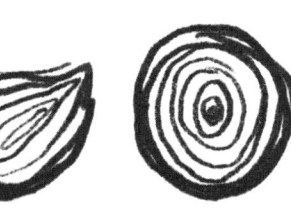

Elizabeth I's, or any twelve-year-old's, wandering all over the page. In that respect he's as grotesque, humorous, tragic and as manifold as any of his creations.

OLIVIER, LAURENCE (later Lord Olivier) was the greatest English actor while I was growing up. In 1939, he was an Oscar-nominated film star, a sexy Heathcliff in *Wuthering Heights*, but his greatest work was done in Shakespeare in the theatre. He married Vivien Leigh (Scarlett O'Hara) in 1940. She was my real clit-twanger, but I do remember meeting him as a schoolgirl collecting autographs at the stage door of the New Theatre, Oxford, when he and second wife Joan Plowright were touring with his great triumph *The Entertainer*. He wore a little brown trilby hat, which he raised when he saw me waiting and I creamed in my knickers on the spot. Many years later, when Joan and I were working in Hollywood together on *I Love You to Death* (1990) I asked her what Sir L was like. She paused; a misty, staring-into-the-past look came into her eyes. She replied: 'He was … animal!' No need for more.

ONE-OFF: Sometimes I do things on impulse. This is a story people ask for, so here it is. In 1962, I was cycling down King's Parade in Cambridge and at the traffic lights I noticed next to me a rather dishy bloke in a convertible. He was blond, tall, an American soldier in uniform (LOVE a uniform!), blue eyes. He

smiled at me and I called out, 'If you follow me to my college, I'll suck you off.' He looked surprised but accepted the offer. The lights changed and off we went. It was mid-afternoon, so no problem with having a man in my room. Up Pfeiffer Arch stairs in Newnham Old Hall we went. There was a little preliminary chat; I asked him where he came from and he replied politely, 'Texas, ma'am'. He told me about his brothers and sisters, I explained I was an only child, and then out popped his member and I fulfilled my promise (I always complete the contract). It seemed to go well, as after zipping up, he said, 'Any chance I can come back next week with some friends from the base?' I refused politely: the wild impulse was gone and sometimes you can overdo things.

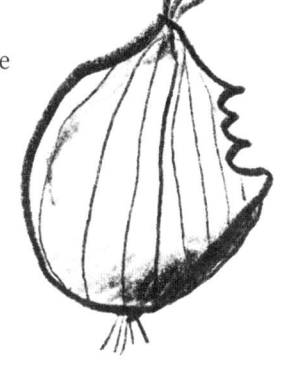

ONIONS: I eat onions like apples, I relish the explosion in the mouth they give (early years of cock-sucking I suppose) – it's a glorious vegetable. Clears the sinuses, keeps people away – useful during pandemics – and has scarcely any calories. And as a metaphor for how to live Life, it's just as useful. Stripping off the layers one by one until you get to the heart – not a bad recipe for personal relationships. I always carry one in my handbag; a non-fattening snack and a conversation-starter.

ONLY CHILD: I was a much-prized, spoilt, golden child; my parents' *only* child, the centre of their worlds. They were determined I should have every advantage they'd been denied. They wanted to make sure I'd be accepted, that no door would be shut to me. And it was a very secure upbringing. I never felt underprivileged. I always knew I was important, because I was to my parents. I don't for a second regret my closeness to them because they gave me so much confidence. The umbilical cord was never completely cut, metaphorically speaking: I still feel connected to them, long after their deaths. It's quite a fate being an only child. I longed for a sibling but the war was on, our Oxford 'hovel' had no room for another, and so I remained single, but so locked in closeness with Mummy and Daddy that we did seem complete. Everything I did fascinated them: I always had their undivided attention and their all-consuming, unconditional adoration. Just the three of us: it was passionate, close, indulgent. It meant that I was ridiculously spoilt, absurdly demanding and selfish, but wonderfully confident that I was profoundly loved. Mummy died in 1974, Daddy in 1995, but their words, their faces, their impact have never left me. Love is what children need more than anything; I had it in buckets.

OPENNESS: When I fell in love with Heather, I wanted to strike the cobwebs away and be my own person. But everybody's different, everybody's caught in the web of their own family and friends. If you live where people loathe homosexuality, or

worse, where being gay is outlawed and forbidden, when you find out that that's who you are, you carry a terrible burden. To be able to release yourself from that burden you need to be able to talk about it. My formidable agent Susan Smith always said you have to know with whom you're having the pleasure; you have to know who you can tell and who is unable to deal with it. I have often talked about my regret at coming out to my parents. But what would have happened to me if I hadn't? I think much of the energy that makes me who I am would have been channelled into playing the part of the virtuous daughter, who had sadly never met the right Jewish doctor. I would have been forced into untruthfulness. I could never have sustained that.

OPERA: When I inherited £6,000 from my mother in 1974, Heather and I decided to buy a house in Italy. To find one, we spent a summer taking bus trips to villages we liked the look of. There we'd hole up in the village bar, armed with our one sentence in Italian: 'We want to buy an unrestored house.' In one bar we met three old men who took us to see a complete wreck and back to their house for wine and cheese. Their farmhouse kitchen was full of labourers eating and drinking and then one wizened worker with terrible teeth stood up to sing. Much to our surprise, his voice was pure and true: Verdi and Puccini poured out into the night air as beautifully as I've ever heard

them. Overcome, I wept. They were terribly worried but then understood. They spoke no English, we no Italian, but opera united us in the most surprising way. It was an epiphany. We didn't buy their house in the end but the memory of his voice still delights me.

ORAL FIXATIONS: Whenever I have found a taste I love, be it Big Tom tomato juice or Bendicks Bittermints (love the macho names!), I have always shared it with the world. Before I realised there was a better option, I kissed a lot of frogs (or penises as they are otherwise known). I roved open-mouthed and increasingly skilled in the art of fellatio through the halls of Academe, not to mention the bike sheds of Newnham – and next morning I relished giving the post-prandial review, blow by blow to the breakfast table of my all-female Cambridge college. My friends were agog, a-gag and frequently hysterical at the latest instalment of my cock-sucking adventures. So, once I discovered clitoral joy in my late twenties, everyone had to be told immediately. I couldn't stay silent; there can never be Too Much Information.

ORGASM: I had my first orgasm when I was eight years old. I was passionately in love with Miss Chase, my form teacher in the Lower Second. One day, walking past her house in Banbury Road with my mother, it happened. I felt a hugely pleasurable heat slowly building in my loins until it was overpowering, leaving me drained, spent. My cunt flooded with juice, just at the thought of her. Just being near her was enough. Afterwards, I was always fascinated by sex. It seemed strange to have such a powerful feeling that went all through your body. There was no friction, it was purely mental. The power of longing and desire. It's been like that ever since. When I saw Heather for the first time, I knew. I don't know how I knew. You look at someone, your groin shifts a bit and you think, 'I FANCY YOU.' Perhaps it's slightly perverse for an eighty-four-year-old to be gassing on about sex so determinedly. But people *should* speak about this, especially women, whose sex drives have been under-acknowledged. Men expect a 'happy ending'; often women are just grateful to have it over. I observed with interest the male emissions I contrived to bring on, orally and off the wrist, and thought how lucky it was that girls didn't 'cream' in quite the same way, needing tissues and towels to wipe up the evidence. I'm not an expert, because I only know my own reactions; but I remember the pleasure of my huge, very early, vaginally-centred hot flush on Banbury Road. Masturbation with a pillow took care of the rest of it, until I was properly fucked by a woman many years later. I've never cared for electrical assistance or equipment. Each to her own. It's worth planning the occasion and my watchword is 'Tits first!'

OSTRICH IMPRESSIONS: In 2024, I was invited by Soho Place Theatre to take part in an intriguing theatrical experiment with Nassim Soleimanpour's *White Rabbit Red Rabbit*. There were no rehearsals, no lines to learn; I just needed to turn up and read the script for the first time in front of a paying audience.

Two days before I was due to walk on stage, I received these instructions.

1. Do not see or read the play beforehand. Learn nothing about it.
2. Prepare an ostrich impression.

Yes – *an ostrich impression*. I am eighty-four and practically crippled by spinal stenosis. Worse, I have no neck (God's oversight) and now I was required to do an ostrich impression without explanation to a full theatre. What on earth was I going to offer the expectant audience? Once I walked on stage I realised after ten seconds that I was being an emu instead – would they notice? Then I morphed into a chicken. My stumpy body contorted itself painfully into one bird after another, a pigeon, a penguin – no ostrich would have recognised me. I flapped my arms, wiggled my bottom (always a winner!), I even squawked a little. They did laugh, thank goodness, possibly more with pity than admiration. And I sat down to generous applause. And now I know I can stick my head back in the sand again.

OUT, COMING: My friend Ian McKellen and I have a constant difference of opinion on this matter. He feels that you should come out as an encouragement to others and be true to yourself. And I said above, it depends who you're coming out to. It hurt my parents too much and it didn't please me particularly, so I think it was an error. I realise now that telling people things that they can't deal with is an indulgence. I believe that if people want to reveal their sexuality they should, but the matter should not be forced. Some people cannot accept their loved ones being homosexual. And if they can't accept it, they shouldn't have to. It's indulgent of those of us who are gay to say you've *got* to know this, you've *got* to share this. I don't think that's right. Of course, it's better if people can be open with the people they love, and talk about it with their family – it's always better if everybody can truly be who they are meant to be – but my insistence on opening up hurt the people I loved most in the world.

OUTRAGEOUS: I know I'm capable of being outrageous, but I don't do it all the time, at home preferring to subside into a book or into the computer. I do not have a public persona; I don't assume sweetness for the camera. I'm the same person no matter where I go or what company I'm in. But, like everyone else, I judge which facet of my personality will suit a particular situation and present it. To that extent, I am calculating – but never to conceal, only to reveal.

OUTSIDER: I'm all the things that make an outsider: a fat homosexual Jew ... My family came from another place to this country, and I don't think you ever forget that. My own life experience has shown me how uncomfortable it is to be the Other – the fat, old, disabled, lesbian Jew is the picture I have of myself, because I think it's the picture I'm shown by the wider world. But I've tried to step outside the box that was made for me. I've tried always to be the 'me' that I liked and enjoyed being. I see myself as friendly, unthreatening, chatty, naturally intelligent but not brainy, loving a laugh, wanting company. And my travelling has taught me that if you present yourself the way you are, and don't pretend to be something else, people of all sorts accept you and behave in a similar way. I may look different, I may sound different, but if you prick me, do I not bleed?

PACIFIC PALISADES: For sixteen years I rented a flat in Santa Monica at the top of the California Incline. Every morning at six, I would drive down Pacific Coast Highway to the Topanga Canyon exit and up into the Palisades YMCA outdoor pool. Set in the hills above Sunset Boulevard and Gelson's delicatessen, the pool was surrounded by trees, just a few houses in sight. Wildlife seemed close and unafraid; deer suddenly visible running on the slopes; if you stood on the deck with an outstretched arm, the blue jay came to be fed by hand, eagles circled above us as we swam. The conversation in the bare concrete Ladies' Locker Room likewise sustained, thrilled, surprised and never disappointed. How we talked, argued and shared. Rachel was a Zionist; Crosby, who died too young of cancer and was related to Bing; Cassidy and Michelle, superb, competitive swimmers; Dot, very committed on the Masters team; and amazing Marie, who continued swimming well into her late eighties.

Chatting to those women, all of us stark naked in the showers, forms my happiest memories of America. I'd never been in a pool with so many Jews, except in Israel. It was twenty-five metres long, immaculately kept, and the swim coaches *Baywatch*-type blokes who were lovely to me even though I didn't know how to do the crawl (we were only taught breaststroke at Oxford High School). Kevin and Michael are still my friends; the sun shone on our oiled bodies, and I was not so fat then so could climb down the steps into the water and swim under the divisions into the slow lane. I knew my place. But when I heard that Gelson's had been burnt down in the recent fires, I knew that not only a whole district but an entire way of life had perished, never to be restored.

PALESTINE: Growing up, I didn't know very much about Palestine; it was my understanding that Israel had won a war and the Jews would survive. And that was good. But little by little, as I became more political, I educated myself. The more I read books and articles about the situation, the more I became critical of Israel.

When I went to Palestine in 2012, I saw for myself the contempt and cruelty with which Israelis treated Palestinians. I met Palestinian people and listened to their personal stories. I saw the devastation of the hospitals that the Israelis had bombed. I saw incredible overcrowding. I saw the filth and stench in the streets of Hebron. I saw the nets that the Arabs have to put up to protect themselves from the settlers who shower them with muck and rubbish. It was a searing experience that really shook me.

The Palestinian people were not being treated in a humane way; they told me how their lives have been disrupted, made miserable; how they had been humiliated, arrested and, most poignant of all, how they had been torn from their homes, and their lands taken away. Their daily lives are being squeezed and destroyed and since they never see Israelis to talk to, they feel a hatred of them. I'm not surprised. I would if I were treated in the same way.

I, as a Jew, have the full right of return – no Palestinian does. It's just not fair. The Israelis feel they can carry through things without reference to international law; what they are doing is illegal. Yet nobody seems to be taking any notice.

If my North London Jewish critics, who lambast me as a 'fascist' and a liar, experienced for themselves the trials of being Palestinian, they might modify their views and perhaps encourage a change of behaviour in Israel. Those Jews, like me, who speak out against the wickedness of the Israeli government, are tarred with the epithet of 'self-hating Jew' – but I will continue to speak out. I have to. I am not optimistic for the future.

PANDA: I saw my first giant panda when filming *The Real Marigold on Tour* in Sichuan province, China. I cried. The extraordinary thing was that the panda was looking back at me. In my whole life I would never have dreamed that I would look at an animal like that and it would return my sympathetic gaze. Tears rolled down my cheeks as I fed it a bamboo shoot. 'So beautiful,' I said, mopping my eyes. 'It's a piece of magic.' But chef and fellow oldie Rosemary Shrager was impassive. 'It's just a panda,' she said with a shrug. But the panda wasn't looking at her.

PARKING: This is a fraught subject because it is a catalogue of scrapes, dents, bangs, a vaginal examination and becoming Mim the Crim for eight hours. If you park in the Sydney Opera House, you may well miss the performance. It's the world's deepest car park, took two years to build and I thought it would take me the same amount of time to find my car. The structure is a double-helix, doughnut-shaped maze, twelve storeys beneath the ground for 1,100 cars. I defy anyone parking there not to need therapy afterwards.

But that scary experience pales into insignificance when compared to one Thursday in London, when I parked on a double-yellow line in busy Shaftesbury Avenue and ran upstairs to deliver a voice-over tape to my agent. It took one minute: when I returned to the car, there was a motorcycle policeman in jackboots, putting a parking ticket on my windscreen. I am afraid I lost my temper: I snatched the ticket off the windscreen, tore it into little pieces and threw them in the air. 'You've got a dick that small!' I shouted, indicating a very small member with my index finger and thumb. That must have hit home.

'Right. Now you get another ticket for breach of the peace and litter.'

'Go on, then! Arrest me! I don't care what you do. I demand to be taken to a police station!'

'Don't worry, Miss. You're going to a police station,' he said.

He radioed for backup. (Did I mention it was the State Opening of Parliament?) Seconds later, three panda cars flashing blue lights screamed up. Six more policemen climbed out and shoved their arms under my armpits and half-lifted, half-frogmarched me across the road, my little legs wriggling in the air. By this time, a crowd of curious onlookers had gathered. I shouted out, 'You see what happens in England?' And then a hand on my head bundled me into the backseat of a police car.

I was taken to Bow Street Police Station, where the station sergeant booked me in and emptied my handbag. A small packet wrapped in silver paper caught his eye. 'Aha! Well, well, well. What have we got here, Miss Margolyes?' He was clearly suspecting drugs.

'If you look closely, Officer, you'll see it's a packet of Trebor peppermints.'

He looked a little deflated; I think my middle-class confidence needled him. He thought, 'I'll show that cocky bitch.' (Yes, I am imagining that's what he thought, because of his next words.) 'Well, nevertheless, you will have to be examined. We don't know who you are,' came the reply.

'What are you talking about? I'm an actress on television!'

'Well,' he said. 'I've never seen you.'

I was locked into a private examination room and told to wait for 'the matron'. I guessed that the matron would give me an intimate physical examination looking for drugs, so I thought I might as well take off all my clothes. When the matron walked in, I was standing there completely naked. She smiled nastily and said, 'You've been here before.'

'I most certainly have not!' I retorted.

'Well, how did you know to take your clothes off?'

'Because I guessed you'd examine me for drugs. And I'm not going to be examined in my clothes,' I told her. 'I'm an actress. I'm used to taking off my clothes.' I had to lie on the examination table while she carried out a vaginal examination. And she also poked me up the arse. Obviously, she came away empty-handed. I put my clothes back on. I was then remanded in custody for eight hours, nearly missing another voice-over. They thought being fingered in the vagina by a woman would distress me. How wrong they were! I thought all my Christmases had come at once.

Parking with my Blue Badge has been a godsend. It rescues me from hours of pain and means the world can be reached, even if I can't walk. I suggest that the bastards who take disabled parking spaces without being disabled are forced to park in Sydney Opera House – wherever they live.

PARTNER: What do you call the person you're not married to? And why do people want to get married anyway? When Heather and I after fifty years together formed a *civil partnership*, it was pragmatic not romantic. Without it, if one of you falls ill, doctors and hospitals are not obliged to tell the other anything. But we have never relished the thought of referring to one another as 'wife'. I don't understand why gay people are so anxious to follow the straights on this. But it doesn't bother me what anyone does, as long as it's legal and no animals are hurt in the process. Life is sweeter shared. Go for it.

PATRIARCHY: Lesbianism did not stop my appreciation of men as people; the men I like, I like a lot. But the Patriarchs have no power over me. I need nothing from men. They cannot bully me. And if they try to threaten me in the street, I have a voice like thunder which I do not scruple to use.

PENIS: This will be a short entry. It has to be short because my acquaintance with the treasured dongle is in the past, was always oral and necessarily fleeting. The only time I have penis envy is when I'm in a car and need to pee. Otherwise, I think it's such an *odd* addendum; I can't imagine what chaps do when it starts to move on its own. And the foreskin sensitivity, coupled with stale smegma, is dazzlingly inefficient. Although brought up Jewish, I am now an opponent of circumcision, unless the male requests it. It doesn't seem right to impose an unnecessary operation on a small baby. Men do worry so about the size – they should rather focus on the skill required to please the receiving vagina. Bit of a selfish organ, I think; like alcohol, penes (*pl.*) should be used responsibly.

PERIOD COSTUMES: A life in corsets was not for me but I gratefully acknowledge the help costume designers and wardrobe mistresses have been throughout my career. I owe most of my acting awards to the costumes they created to enable my characters to come to life. I'm thinking of Madame Morrible (*Wicked*) Mrs Mingott (*The Age of Innocence*) and Flora Finching (*Little Dorrit*), who really started my whole film career. Christine Edzard, the brilliant director who had been Franco Zeffirelli's set designer, *personally* measured and fitted me for Flora Finching. She knew how crucial it is to make every costume express the character's life. And the strange thing is I've never seen her wear anything but dark blue corduroy trousers and a dark blue jumper.

Perhaps the only advantage of excess flesh is that it encourages mirth. Costume designers over the years rejoiced in my belly, double chins and bosoms, deliberately accentuated the continental shelves of mammary excess, straining for release from the highly decorative fabrics they sourced lovingly from across the world.

PERIODS: I was the first person in my class to have periods; I was eleven. Mummy wrote a note to tell the school of my startling female development. I was summoned to see Miss West, our games mistress, who had the unfortunate duty of discussing the matter with all who menstruated. She was one of the Oxford High School lesbians and always wore divided skirts. She was extremely embarrassed by the whole thing … I turned up wondering what I'd done wrong.

Miss West gave an awkward snigger and said, 'Miriam, I think we must have a little chat about how to, er … manage your periods.' I could see she was embarrassed; I wasn't at all. Miss West took a deep breath and resolutely continued. 'In the pavilion … there are no, er … incinerators. So, on the days when we are playing hockey and you have your, er … period, I am afraid you will have to bring some newspaper to school and [*snigger*] wrap your ... er ... sanitary towel in a newspaper and, er ... take it home [*snigger*] ... in your satchel.'

Possibly I was the first one that had to face that conversation; before, when people had periods, they simply didn't play hockey. But many years later my version of Miss West reappeared in an episode of *Jam and Jerusalem* at the express request of Jennifer Saunders. I hope Miss West was not revolving in her grave. She was only doing her best in excruciating circumstances.

P

PG TIPS: From about 1978, all the way through to the mid-eighties, I recorded a good number of the famous PG Tips adverts with the chimpanzees. I was Dolly, who had a charlady voice, while Ada, the other chimp (whose real name was Choppers), was Stanley Baxter. Nowadays you couldn't do it because they used real chimpanzees from Twycross Zoo, who were dressed up and filmed drinking tea and so on. In one of our ads, Dolly was at the sink up to her elbows in suds, when she says, 'I'm fed up with this washing-up. My Phil always calls me his little dishwasher.' Then Stanley, playing Ada, replies, 'What do you call him, then?' and I reply, 'Bone idle!' At the end of each commercial, Dolly would have a swig of Brooke Bond's PG Tips, and say, 'It's the taste.'

POCKETS: I don't envy men much but they do get pockets right. Pockets are essential in my life, and every garment I own must have them. All my frocks have them and my costume designers respect this. Why do men's clothes have endless pockets, women's hardly any? I'm going to have it in my contract in future: 'No pockets, no show.'

POLITICS: I've become more political as I've got older; I haven't mellowed – I've billowed. The world has changed and I've had to change with it. I make no apology. Innocence has evaporated; naked greed and power-hungry billionaires control our press, our elections and our future. It's the fault of the left that the right and extreme right are triumphing. In America, the Supreme Court Justice Ruth Bader Ginsburg should have resigned to make way for someone younger; Obama didn't see the threat; Biden should not have been a candidate; Kamala Harris didn't stand a chance – and the Republicans have been systematically preparing the courts for a take-over. My books and my one-woman shows reflect my mindset. Palestine and Zionism and Trump fill my thoughts and enrage me – Farage waiting in the wings to become prime minister and the rise of fascism in the UK ever more apparent. Of course I'm more political, what do you expect? Follow my example and save the world. Be awoken!

'POPULAR' CULTURE: Sorry, I'm an intellectual snob not really interested in popular culture, culture on its own does it for me. In the sixties, when I was growing up and pop culture was at its height, I scorned it, so all that terrific music and vitality and fashion passed me by. I was a 'swot': I read books and went to the theatre, the opera, classical music concerts – and I survived! But I was wrong: I should have looked around me and given all those new things a chance. Mummy loved the high and the low – Conchita Supervia and Max Miller, Margot Fonteyn and George Formby, Ralph Richardson and Gracie Fields – Shakespeare and Tommy Handley. And now I see the error of closing eyes and ears to the less elevated expression of the human condition. We can all enjoy and experience the high and the low culture; there's no requirement to make it for one class or educational level than for another. I didn't 'get' Bob Dylan or The Doors or The Rolling Stones or Andy Warhol. More fool me!

POTATOES: To the slender, potatoes are just another vegetable. But to fatties like me, they're fraught with danger; they're emotional, they cause fights, they can cause death. And to make matters worse, they're delicious in almost any recipe. Latkes are top of the tops, but I enjoy potatoes in their jackets, mashed, roasted (with or without goose fat), dauphinoise, German *Kartoffelsalat ohne Speck*; just plain-boiled Jersey Royals are gorgeous too. Robertson, where I live in Australia, has a famous giant potato in the Main Street; tourists come to photograph it. But that's not the reason I live there, although Robertson potatoes are famous throughout New South Wales.

Potatoes both comfort and frighten me: forbidden fruit bursting with taste and calories. Mummy was too fat and she knew it. Daddy and I were always trying to stop her from having too many potatoes. On one occasion, when I tried to stop Mummy from having a second helping of potatoes for supper, we had a terrible row. I threw her plate full of roast spuds to the floor and rushed out. I ran down Banbury Road – a very long road – all the way down to St Giles's Church near the Martyrs' Memorial. I collapsed on a grave in the churchyard and sat there for hours, weeping uncontrollably. I walked home. It was all for nothing – Mummy had finished the potatoes.

POTTER, HARRY:

>**Prof. Sprout:** Morning, everyone. Good morning, everyone! Welcome to Greenhouse Three, second years. Now gather around, everyone. Today we're going to re-pot mandrakes. Who here can tell me the properties of the mandrake root? Yes, Miss Granger?
>
>**Hermione Granger:** Mandrake, or mandragora, is used to return those who have been petrified to their original state. It's also quite dangerous. The mandrake's cry is fatal to anyone who hears it.
>
>**Prof. Sprout:** Excellent, ten points to Gryffindor. Now, as our mandrakes are still only seedlings, their cries won't kill you yet, but they could knock you out for several hours, which is why I've given each of you a pair of earmuffs – for auditory protection. So, could you please put them on right away. Quickly! Flaps tight down and watch me closely. You grasp your mandrake firmly, you pull it sharply over the pot ... got it! ... and now you dunk it down into the other pot and pour a little sprinkling of soil to keep him warm. Oh, Longbottom's been neglecting his earmuffs.
>
>**Seamus Finnigan:** No, ma'am, he's just fainted.
>
>**Prof. Sprout:** [*sighs*] Yes, well, just leave him there. [*Pause.*] Right, on we go! Plenty of pots to go around. Grasp your mandrake, and pull it up.

All the children on set were impeccably behaved, possibly a tad prim, and they decided that every time I said 'fuck', or some other 'bad word', I had to put ten pence into a swear jar, the proceeds of which would go to the World Wildlife Fund. I don't know how much the obscenity fund amounted to in the end, but it was an appreciable sum.

I'm sure that Harry Potter's world is a good world. But it's not my world. It's like this: I have to step gingerly over the gap between the Harry Potter world and mine, and hope that you'll understand that despite the fact that I'm head of Hufflepuff and you're in Gryffindor, I don't really want to talk about Harry Potter any more.

P

PRANKS: At Oxford High School, in Miss Willett's French class, I dressed up as a French lady who had come to inspect the school for her daughter. I borrowed Mummy's best fur coat and her court shoes, and I tripped into the classroom, saying in a very thick French accent, 'Oh, I'm zo veery sorry to interrupt everyzing. I am veery interested in how you teach ze French in ze school.' I rolled my *r*'s in a pretty good approximation of a French accent. The whole class was writhing with laughter, and even Miss Willetts tried not to smile as she said, 'Come along, Miriam, you're wasting time.' To which I replied, 'Oh, zo you do not vant me to stay? Well, zen, I will go.' And with a flounce of Mummy's fur coat, I stepped out into the hall (and into yet another detention).

PROBATION: I once visited a well-run women's prison in Virginia. I met two young recidivist offenders – drug addicts who'd been repeatedly convicted of thieving. I talked to them for quite a long time; I told them the truth: that they were both beautiful and intelligent, and that they could and must do more with their lives than spend them in prison. 'I know that you've got a contribution to make,' I said. These two young women told me that nobody had ever talked to them as if they were human, or as if there was any potential there for a better life. I found that remarkable and sad. I don't know if it made a difference to their fate after they were released: drugs were the way of life there; they were addicts and it would have been very hard for them to break away from their social environment – but they were incredibly grateful that I had spent time with them, looked into their eyes and talked to them about themselves. Many people need that, and that's why I still think I might have made a good probation officer. I like to think of myself sitting behind a desk, looking into a criminal's eyes, and making them see that there was a future beyond prison.

PROMPT: I was in my First Year at Cambridge, performing Lorca's *Blood Wedding* at the ADC. Without warning, my mind became a blank; I stared at the other actors; we looked helplessly for some agonising moments at each other. I turned to the Stage Manager in the wings, but there was no joy to be had there. She was fanning through the pages of the script, having clearly lost her place, if not the plot, and there was no help for it but to rush off stage, down to my dressing room, rootle around for my script, find the page, run back upstairs, hurtle onto the stage and *say the line*. I couldn't look at my fellow actors, who were glassy with terror and embarrassment. God knows how they filled in the time when I was 'off'. I apologised, of course, but I don't think they ever forgave me.

PRUNES AND PRISMS: Miss Prism in *The Importance of Being Earnest* is a part I was born to play – a rotund, respectable English governess, barely containing her violent, boiling sexuality. She has wit ('The good ended happily, and the bad unhappily. That is what Fiction means') and a guileless, single-minded determination to snaffle her man.

Unfortunately, there was a problem. The object of my character's passion, as conceived by Oscar Wilde, was a mild, sexually repressed country vicar, the Reverend Chasuble. But Terence Rigby, the actor cast as Chasuble in this particular production, said, 'No, no, no. Chasuble is not interested in Prism. I mean, there's nothing going on between them.' But it's crystal-clear from the text that there is. This play specifically is about setting up couples. They may not be the sort of couples that one would have in mind – elderly and not particularly attractive, in our case – but the work is supposed to be a celebration of unbridled love. So there I was, acting my part, but with an actor who was not prepared to act *his*.

The phrase 'prunes and prisms' is meant to encapsulate a repressed, pent-up kind of person. Well, that's Miss Prism to a T, and that's why Oscar Wilde called her that. My Miss Prism positively throbbed with sexual longing. I didn't allow Terence to deflect me from the passage of my lust. That's the point. She may be a governess, she may be tightly laced, but that doesn't mean that her cunt isn't flowing with desire. So, there was I, boiling with love and lust and not able to pass it on to my recalcitrant Dr Chasuble. He spent every night running away from me across the stage whilst I remained a pressure cooker, steaming towards him – and the more repressed Terry wanted to be, the more I seethed out at him. And it worked.

Miss Prism: You are too much alone, dear Dr Chasuble. You should get married. A misanthrope I can understand – a womanthrope, never!

Chasuble: [*with a scholar's shudder*] Believe me, I do not deserve so neologistic a phrase. The precept as well as the practice of the Primitive Church was distinctly against matrimony.

Miss Prism: [*sententiously*] That is obviously the reason why the Primitive Church has not lasted up to the present day. And you do not seem to realise, dear Doctor, that by persistently remaining single, a man converts himself into a permanent public temptation. Men should be more careful; this very celibacy leads weaker vessels astray.

Chasuble: But is a man not equally attractive when married?

Miss Prism: No married man is ever attractive except to his wife.

Chasuble: And often, I've been told, not even to her.

Miss Prism: That depends on the intellectual sympathies of the woman. Maturity can always be depended on. Ripeness can be trusted. Young women are green.

QUANTOCKS: I think it's a part of Somerset, but I love the sound and decided it would be a terrific addition to my collection of swear words. It involves the back of the throat, it's explosive and sounds vaguely insulting. 'You're a real Quantock, you are!' What do you think?

QUARREL, NEVER LET THE SUN SET ON A: Everyone asks me for advice, especially about relationships, because I've been lucky enough to have enjoyed a lasting love for fifty-eight years. But we're all different – how can I advise anyone who lives in a different way? I'm no psychologist. I do have one stock response, however, which I believe in and use myself. Never let the sun set on a quarrel. Don't go to bed, stiff with resentment and rage, going over in your head the rotten things you hurled at each other earlier. Look straight into the other's eyes, hold out your arms and say, 'I love you and I'm sorry.' No other words are needed.

QUEEN: I was a passionate royalist as a child; my den was plastered with photos of HMQ from floor to ceiling; and the Coronation was the peak. I remember the night of 2 June 1953, standing at my bedroom window in Banbury Road, Oxford, gazing out over the garden. It had been a vivid day at our lovely neighbour Mrs Harwood's, first watching the whole thing on her TV (we didn't have one then), followed by fending off a dirty young man, who groped me and then attempted a tongue-down-the-throat kiss. I gave him short shrift because what mattered was Her Majesty coming out of the Abbey, serious and slender, getting into the State Coach with all her soaked subjects cheering, and I said aloud, 'This is Coronation Day, and you must remember it all your life.' And I have.

QUEER: Originally meaning peculiar, strange and eccentric, 'queer' is the word I now use to describe my sexual orientation. But it wasn't always so. When I was growing up, the word was 'homosexual'. Or 'pansy' or 'faggot' or 'shirt-lifter'. 'Dyke' or 'lesbo' were reserved for us girls. It was considered a term of abuse. And then, sometime in the 1970s, it seemed to change. 'Gay' took over and there was quite a fuss. Folk complained in the papers that a lovely word, redolent of jolly japes and innocent picnics, was being misused. But language adapts and moves about. In a trice, 'queer' was back, defiant, and I happily answer to that. After all, 'straight' is hardly a compliment.

QUEUING is a peculiarly English habit that we're all proud of. In fact, I can become violent if I see queue-jumping; it deeply offends my sense of fairness. It started during the war and friendships were struck up during queues and kindnesses done when people had to leave and return – 'save a place for me' was the watchword. The NHS now has a queuing system all its own; waiting lists go into the millions. I blame the Tories for that, as I blame them for almost everything.

In Italy, they don't queue, but they have such a commitment to a civilised routine at the market stall that everyone knows who's in front of them and there are seldom any nasty moments.

You have to work out what's worth queuing for. Food at certain places definitely is; the Beigel Shop in Brick Lane and Nardulli's **ICE CREAM** parlour at Clapham Common I can understand. Kids queued at midnight for the Harry Potter volumes to come out – quaint but not for me. I've queued all night twice in my life: for **BURTON AND TAYLOR** and for Maria Callas's *Tosca* at the Royal Opera House. It was worth it on both occasions. I won't queue for the loo. And it is monstrous that there are never enough Ladies' loos; I have no scruples in taking over the Gents if necessary. It's fun actually – the chaps look so scared when I blunder in. But many blokes are kind and volunteer their loos when clearly the crush is beyond repair. The queues I relish are the ones for my book tours; it's really heartening to feel popular, and I wave as I get wheeled in at the stage door. I never forget that fans are the backbone of our industry.

QUIET, BE: This is a favourite story of mine. I don't think I come out of it particularly well but the tale of how I finally got to meet my childhood idol is a funny one. It was British Book Week and I was thrilled to have been invited to the reception at Buckingham Palace. Smiling equerries guided us to the enormous red and gold reception hall where hundreds of people thronged and buzzed. I knew somewhere in there the queen was mingling. I approached one of the equerries. 'Excuse me, would it be possible for me to meet the queen? I would so love to.'

'Oh, perfectly possible. You simply locate Her Majesty in this mêlée, form a semicircle, smile, and if Her Majesty sees you smiling in her direction, she will approach and talk to you.'

We immediately spotted the queen, looking exactly as she should, with a helmet of iron-grey hair and her handbag clamped like a grenade to her elbow. We shuffled into a semicircle of three, using a Trooping the Colour technique, and smiled like billy-o, pasting rictus grins onto our faces. And almost immediately, Her

Majesty turned and came towards us; others soon followed to join our semicircle. And then Her Majesty the Queen was standing in front of me. 'And what do *you* do?' she asked. Instead of saying like any normal person, 'Your Majesty, I am an actress who records audio books,' I took a deep breath, and declared, 'Your Majesty, I am the best reader of stories in the whole world!' There was a pause. The queen looked at me with dislike, rolled her eyes heavenwards, sighed and turned to the man standing beside me. 'And what do *you* do?'

He replied, 'Your Majesty, I'm an academic trying to help dyslexic children to read. We've discovered that if the letters on the page are printed in different colours and if the pages themselves, the paper, is of different colours, it helps the children to absorb the information more quickly and easily.'

I couldn't help joining in. 'My goodness, how fascinating!' I said loudly. 'I didn't know that.'

Her Majesty swivelled sharply back to me and said, 'Be quiet!' The *t* of 'quiet' was especially crisp.

QUESTIONNAIRE: The following can spice up the dullest dinner-party:

1. When did you have your first fuck?
2. How long do you want to live?
3. Your biggest mistake?
4. Your greatest triumph?
5. What enrages you about modern life?
6. The greatest sin?
7. Is religion useful?
8. Should inequality of income be abolished?

9. Create an alternative Ten Commandments.
10. Is space travel a waste of space?
11. Who should define madness?
12. Should cunnilingus be taught in schools?
13. Do you prefer to look forwards or backwards?
14. Best Jewish joke?
15. Would you change sex?
16. Why did you marry your partner?
17. Are you born in the wrong century?
18. Are you antisemitic?
19. Should obesity be a punishable offence? (Daddy thought so.)
20. Is the Country always better than the City?
21. Has America's legacy bettered or worsened human happiness?
22. What's the greatest compliment you've been given?
23. Was it justified?
24. What laws have you broken?
25. Who benefits most from anal sex?

But use with care. I once asked a table full of chums to share their most shocking moment. A demure guest surprised us all with her story of having sex in the department store window she'd just dressed; and then a series of jaw-dropping stories rolled out until finally a quiet voice said: 'Discovering my children hate me' – and, well that was the end of the evening.

QUESTIONS, ASKING: I have always asked lots of questions. My technique is friendly but direct; I go for the jugular and ask the questions I think people don't want to answer. Thus, a good question to start balls rolling is: 'When did you have your first fuck?' Jay Rayner reminded me of the first time we met. I sat down at the Rayner kitchen table, looked under it, and said to his brother Adam: 'Darling, what enormous feet you have. Do you have a huge cock?' I can't help myself, it's natural rudery. But it's not *just* that. I also truly believe it relaxes people, because they unite in being appalled. There is such a thrill in getting a totally unrehearsed reaction. You learn more about the people you are talking to. And I was genuinely curious. Questions demand answers. Asking a question is not just accepting someone else's statements: it's probing, curious, *interested*. It's one of the foundations of Jewish education; we call it *pilpul*.

QUIDDITCH: My memories of the whole Harry Potter experience come in flashes of scenes and moments. In one scene we had to play Quidditch; a bizarre experience, because it was all done on 'green screen'. We had to stand stock-still by a pole against a green background. We each had a number, and when somebody called your number, you had to make a gesture of some kind, as if the elusive and darting Golden Snitch was right there at the end of your nose. I was decidedly non-committal about Quidditch; the sport didn't make my blood race at all. I remember determinedly swiping with my Quidditch stick at an imaginary Golden Snitch and becoming quite red in the face and sweaty with my exertions. Funnily enough, my former next-door neighbour became the president of the UK Quidditch Society – though they play on bicycles rather than broomsticks.

QUOLL AMBASSADOR: Whenever anybody asks me to help refugees, or to support the legalisation of euthanasia, or campaign to protect the environment, or raise money for a theatre at risk, I sign up immediately. However, such impulsiveness can have repercussions. For example, I'd never heard of the spotted-tail quoll when I agreed to be its ambassador. The quoll is a small nocturnal marsupial mammal in danger of extinction, only found in Australia. (It appealed to me because I'm also a small mammal in imminent danger of extinction.) Quoll are often confused with another Australian mammal also under threat, the quokka – even harder to protect. While much admired for their furry smiling face, the quokka are no good in a crisis: faced with imminent danger they just hurl their babies at the approaching predator. While no particular fan of children, I do think that's going a bit far.

'QUOTH THE RAVEN': As a young actress on tour, the digs we ended up in varied a great deal. Luckily, they all had a well-thumbed visitors' book – which, of course, we used to rummage through to find out if it was a good place to stay. The remarks from previous guests had their own discreet shorthand. The one to really look out for was 'Quoth the Raven', code for the warning: 'To be avoided at all costs'. We actors all knew the full line from Edgar Allan Poe's poem: 'Quoth the Raven, "Nevermore."' That clinched it.

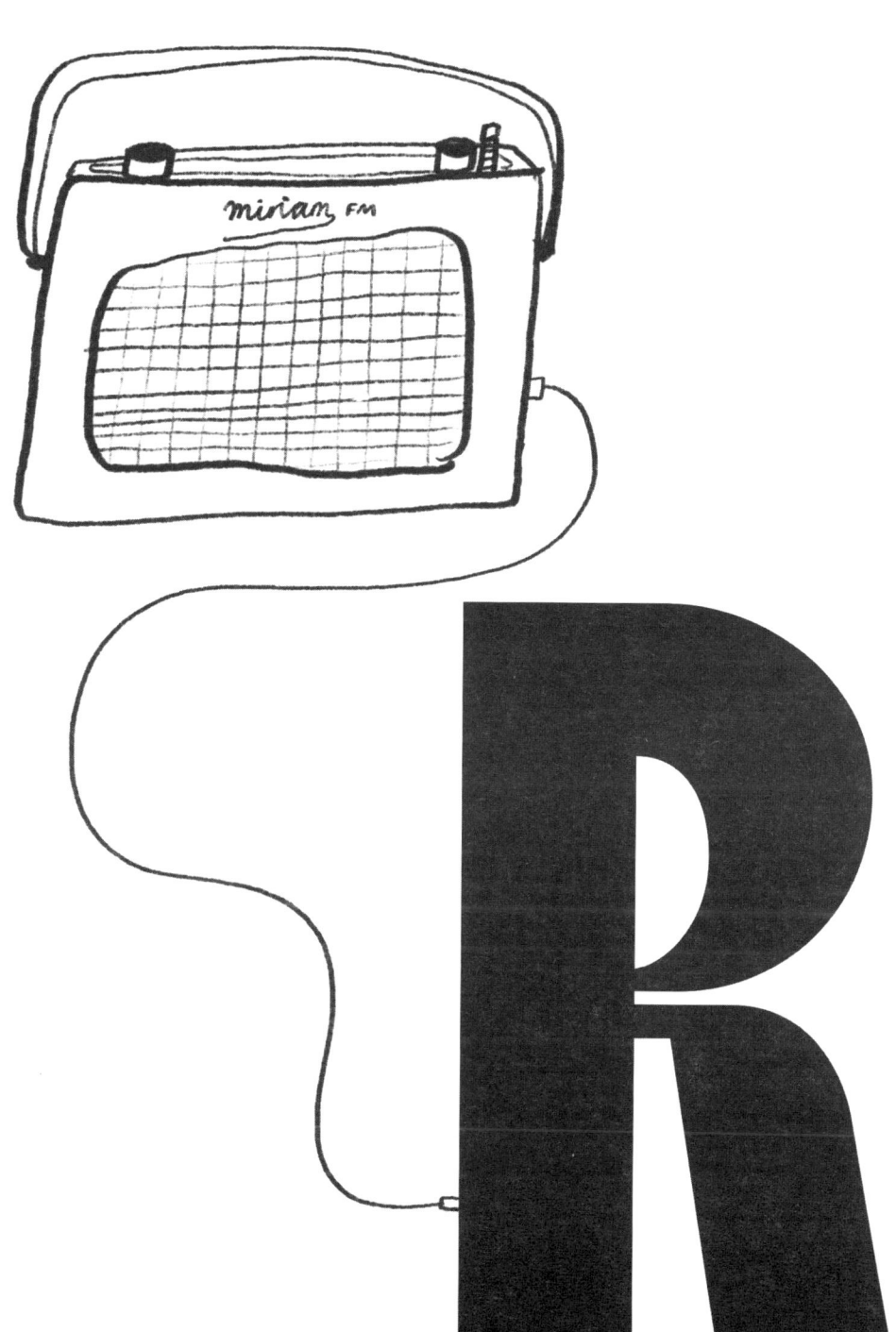

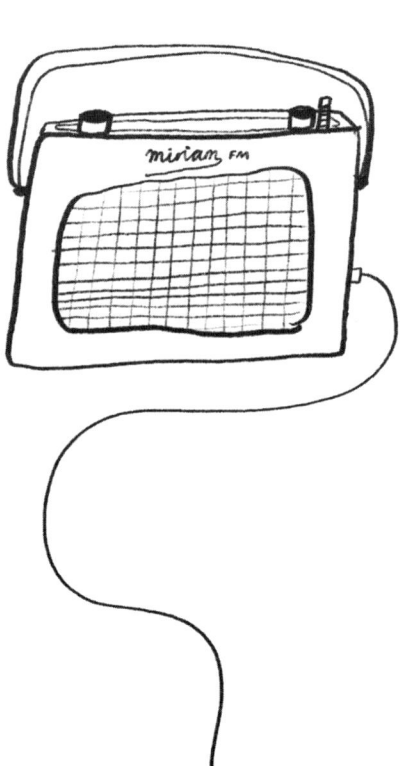

RABBIS: It's hard to explain what a rabbi is. Rabbis are not priests; they are teachers and students at the same time; learned, always, and respected leaders of their communities – rather like a Mafia consigliere. Judaism was a rigidly male domain. I still feel weird when I stand in front of the Torah, as if I have no right to be there. I've known some smashers in three continents, both women and men. My first rabbi was Rav Samuel Daiches. Daddy was his doctor and we loved him; he was immensely learned, gregarious, warm, chubby and fun. They remained family friends and we visited them often after he retired to Cricklewood, always bringing Mummy's fried fish, which he particularly relished. Rabbi Daiches was followed into the Oxford Hebrew Congregation by Rav Jacob Weinberg; my father was also his family doctor and I'm happy to say I'm still good friends with both his daughters, although they know I am no longer a believer. When Rabbi Weinberg left Oxford in 1948 for Muizenberg, South Africa, Rav Chaim Rabin replaced him. Batya, his adorable wife, taught *cheder* (Sunday School), and when they left for Israel, we remained in contact, and I stayed with Batya in their home in Rehavia, Jerusalem, after Chaim had died. She had forgiven me for being such a bad student of Hebrew. Jonathan Keren-Black, my rabbi in Melbourne, is British-born, endlessly kind, and tries hard to bring his more conservative congregation to broaden their attitudes; and my local Chabad rabbi, Moshe Adler, is the most inclusive, hard-working young father you could wish for. He fixed the *mezuzah* on my Clapham house and constantly checks on me, to make sure I'm still all right. And I must mention my extraordinary cousin, Rabbi Roddy Young, who only found out he was Jewish when he was twenty-one, lives with his partner Zolli in Norfolk, has a house in Tuscany and is hospitable, a brilliant orator, thoughtful and deeply modern.

I have known two women rabbis in my life, both remarkable. While I lived in Santa Monica, I listened to the sermons of Rabbi Naomi Levy. I didn't meet her, but I admired her. Inclusivity is what I am seeking, recognition that no man (or woman) is an island. I found it in her sermons. The second woman rabbi is Julia Neuberger. Ten years younger than me, she was a brilliant scholar at my college and is now a baroness and one of the leading Jews in the UK. She is happily married, has a lovely family, is a truly magnificent hostess; her Passover *Seder* Night suppers are packed and the conversation is certainly the best in Hampstead.

How different they all are, but enriched by the Jewish tradition which binds even the most unwilling. The rabbi for my life, however, was Michael Roth, who led Beth Ohr, a liberal reconstructionist synagogue in the Valley, LA. His powerful humanity, entrancing sense of humour and passionate care for us, his congregation, were outstanding. When I confided to him my lack of faith, he said, 'Miriam, don't worry, I don't know if I believe in God, either. Who knows? But for me, it's better that I do, so I carry on.' I don't know any other rabbi who would say that. He had a wisdom and open-mindedness that was both reassuring *and* illuminating.

That's what you long for in a rabbi.

RADIO: I was from the last generation to be brought up on radio, listening to the BBC Home Service. It is the most perfect performance medium. You focus on the voice and if you get it right, job done. Norman Wright, who auditioned me in 1964, told me it was the best audition he'd ever judged. I'm still thrilled to know that. I was offered a job with the BBC Drama Repertory Company in 1965; that was certainly the beginning of my professional life. It was truly the golden age of radio, and great actors were glad to share their acting skills with novices like me, along with such veteran broadcasters like Marjorie Westbury, Malcolm Hayes, Norman Shelley and Carleton Hobbs (after whom the radio prize is named). In those early days, you stood on either side of the microphone and looked into the eyes of the actor opposite. Later, the technology developed and we actors found ourselves on the same side of the mike; the sound might have been better, but it was much harder to achieve the connection between us, to ignite the creative spark which makes radio such a joy. It was in radio that I became an actress. I'm always at home in a radio studio: I know what I'm doing and what I *want* to do. It's probably where I'll end up, but if Fate decrees radio is my last job, I will be sad – but eternally grateful.

RADISH: When asked which I prefer – radishes or sex – I said if it was *good* sex, then I'd rather have sex. But if it was *bad* sex ... I'd rather have a radish. No contest!

RAISING THE FALLEN: Breasts have always loomed large in my life. I realised at an early age, from remarks made by teachers and school friends, that the two bumps on the front of my body had an impact somehow stronger than my feet or my shoulders. At eleven years old, I was a 36B cup – equal to that of my Domestic Science teacher. And they have only got bigger. Eventually I decided that I needed to call the experts. And the leading experts at Raising the Fallen are Rigby & Peller, lingerie and swimwear supplier to the richest, whose Royal Warrant was removed after their founder, June Kenton, former bra-fitter to the queen, referenced her trips to Buckingham Palace in her autobiography, *Storm in a D-Cup*.

I recently mentioned to my friend Eileen Atkins that I had made an appointment with R & P and, to my amazement, she said she'd come too. If you're a frequent flyer with R & P, as she is, you have a permanent measurement with them (like Mummy did at the Oxford New Theatre – a permanent seat) and so can easily get an appointment. I thought it might be amusing for the staff to have to deal in one afternoon both with Eileen's perfectly pert and normal-sized breasts and my unbalanced, huge and rapidly descending globes of glory.

Amidst discreet lighting, three welcoming young ladies, and fitting rooms at the back, I was eager to throw myself into the experience of a new bra – a new world of sophisticated breast-trammelling – and volunteered to be measured. I stood there, in my Triumph 'Doreen' bra, size 44DD. 'Doreen' first exploded onto the brassiere market in 1967 and conquered the world; the Arc de Triomphe was the inspiration for the company name. I think I've been wearing it since then and warmly recommend it if you don't need under-wiring. But now – I very much do. I'd hoped for a front-fastening brassiere, but in my case, this couldn't do the job of both supporting my breasts and giving me a more flattering shape. We decided that the aptly named 'Primadonna' Deauville size 44F (designed in Belgium, made in Tunisia) hit the spot – except for the wire underneath the cups. It stuck out at the cleavage point, changing the actual shape. It was clear that was the answer; Primadonna for me! Rigby & Peller know the power of a well-fitting foundation garment, and how it can change how you feel about yourself, how you stand, how you confront the world. It can be done; I urge you all, whatever your age: be brave and have a go.

As time went by, however, a problem emerged. I could not fasten Primadonna on my own. Before, I had stepped into 'Doreen', pulled her over my knickers, up and up, and then struggled successfully through the arm straps and got them onto my shoulders. It was a struggle but it could be done. Primadonna could only be fastened with assistance. This hadn't been a problem until I left London. In London I have two lodgers (Emily and George), my housekeeper Marina (three times a week) and Denise my PA (once a week). There is also my gardener, Marcos, who fills in when necessary – nothing fazes him, except cruelty to flowers.

However, now here in Tuscany, I'm letting everything hang out. I could ask Heather, but we don't get up at the same time, so I just put on my top clothes and don't look in the mirror. My friend Lucy Darwin reminded me of the Ivor Cutler poem:

> If your breasts are too big
> you will fall over –
> unless you wear a rucksack.

We will have to see how things develop.

REBELLION: Rebellion is an essential therapeutic moral force. Rebellions should not be put down; rather, they should be put *up*. Especially now when, throughout the world, we are being threatened by powerful, evil scoundrels. I have not been enough of a rebel; now in my eighties, I want to take on the Baddies and urge you to do the same. Don't settle for less. Bad marriage? Get out. Bad teacher? Find an alternative. Bad dentist? Bite off their fingers!

REDS (NOT IN THE BED): St Margaret's, near Twickenham, will always hold precious memories for me; it's where I turned down a fuck with Warren Beatty. He was filming *Reds* there in 1980 and as he was co-writer, director and lead actor, his time was limited.

I was called for an interview which I was told could only happen in his trailer at lunchtime. According to his biographer, Mr Beatty has had sex with 12,775 women (a number he disputes). On that day in 1980, I knew he was ferociously talented and devastatingly attractive; I knew I was ferociously talented, devastatingly unattractive and standing outside his trailer door at lunchtime. I knocked. Mr Beatty opened the door, looked me up and down and up again and said quite pleasantly, 'Do you fuck?' 'Yes,' I replied, 'but not you,' 'Why is that?' he asked. 'Because I am a lesbian and I fuck girls', I said. (Actually, I prefer to receive as they say in tennis, but I was slightly caught on the hop.) He grinned and said, 'Can I watch?' I replied, 'Pull yourself together and let's get on with the interview.' All this at the door! We went inside, he was charming and professional and I got the job! It wasn't a huge part (mine not his!) but I am in several shots as the Secretary of the Communist Party and had a wonderful time filming in Manchester. We met again in Budapest in 2003 where Annette Bening (his wife) was starring in *Being Julia*. They invited me to supper; it was a joyous reunion. They're still both devastatingly attractive and ferociously talented. NO REGRETS.

REGRETS: It was only after I had slept with Heather that I told my mother that I was gay. I went home to Oxford one weekend and told Mummy, who immediately told my father. I don't think they really believed it. They were not sophisticated. They didn't understand how I could possibly love another woman in *that* way;

it had no reality for them – it was nonsense, it was a perversion. They couldn't regard it as an emotion worthy of mature consideration. My parents knew that it was *possible*, but they didn't think it was possible for *their* Miriam. Miriam wasn't going to be like that because Miriam was perfect, and to be a lesbian was *imperfection*, and so it simply couldn't be entertained for one moment. It also meant that I would never have a nice Jewish husband, and therefore they would never have grandchildren. I think that was part of their sorrow, or disbelief.

Mummy couldn't handle it. She was an extraordinary, incredibly capable woman who loved theatre, opera and music; a many-sided individual, but closed-minded about homosexuality where her daughter was concerned: it was shameful – people weren't supposed to do that sort of thing. It wasn't *proper*. She and my father insisted I come into the drawing room and swear on the Torah that I would never have relations with a woman again. I did as they asked, but I broke my promise. I stayed with Heather because I loved her, because my whole soul cleaved to her: it would have been impossible to stop. And because, somewhere along the line, I knew they were making an unreasonable request.

I still regret that I told them. I knew I couldn't change what I was but I shouldn't have told them.

RELATIONSHIP: Heather and I are often asked for our recipe for a successful relationship. We met in what is now a ridiculously old-fashioned way, through our mutual friend Katerina Clark. Since 1968 we've maintained a long-distance relationship. It's important to find ways of being together but also separate. For many years, two great English writers and lovers, Margaret Drabble and Michael Holroyd, lived at different ends of London from each other – one in Hampstead, one in Ladbroke Grove. I always thought that that was a perfect arrangement.

We are both busy, professional women, and our jobs matter to us: I have to be in an English-speaking country; she has to be where the archives of the Dutch East India Company are available, so she settled in Amsterdam. We decided to give up nothing, to stay together, have separate establishments in separate countries, meet when we could and have the best of both worlds. We're fiercely independent and very different: we each need our own space. I like to be with people but she prefers solitude; she is reserved, quiet, a historian and a scholar, engrossed in her own intellectual world. And, as you know, I am a noisy actress. We are astonishingly different. And this works for us.

I do believe in continuous communication. We phone EVERY DAY at least once, sometimes more. Often quite late at night.

Never stop working on your relationship. I know I could never survive without Heather; I know there could never be a more perfect person for me. This is not to say that it's easy. It is not, and of course we have fierce disagreements. Heather is very clear-eyed, both about me and our relationship. She is loyal in the sense that I know she loves me, but she also sees my faults, with a sometimes pulverising clarity. My friends allow me to behave badly. Heather won't.

RESTRAINT: When you're Jewish, emotion is very close to the surface. I don't have a stiff upper lip; mine is always wobbling and trembling.

RETAIL VIOLENCE: When my mother left school at fourteen, she went to work as a salesgirl in my grandmother's shop. She was a born saleswoman, but only once had to resort to violence. At the end of a day when she'd sold nothing, a woman came into the shop. The woman tried on hat after hat; Mummy was losing patience but was determined to make a sale. Finally she jammed one on the customer's head and twisted it harshly to get the decoration to the front. The woman screamed, tore the hat off and shouted as she ran out, 'Don't come here! They do people in!'

RETIRE, DON'T: Jews don't believe in reincarnation. We are *here* and *now*, and it's up to us to use what we have. To me, retirement is similarly meaningless. I've worked harder as I've got older. Being overworked and filling my life to the brim has kept me going. I look outwards, not inwards. People stimulate me, and there's a constant influx in my life of newness – seeing new places and learning interesting new things. I'm never bored, and I believe that's the secret to a happy and fruitful old age.

RIDER: A 'rider' is the clause in the contract which specifies what you insist on having in your dressing room. Mine is not complicated: give me wi-fi, good brown bread, butter, smoked salmon responsibly sourced, freshly sliced onions and Big Tom

tomato juice and I'm happy. A gin and tonic is always welcome too. Some artists require complete redecoration of the room or bowls of blue M&Ms but I think that's just silly. The most vital thing is having a loo within reach, but that's taken for granted. Going on tour is hard work but also fun and I enjoy the discovery of playing to a new audience in a new theatre in a new town. I am old and new at the same time. Lucky me!

ROLY-POLY: If there's one adjective I loathe, it's 'roly-poly' and it's the one most usually applied to me. When I started appearing on stage and in film and television, I spent a lot of time in corsets because I was often cast in period drama. And the problem with corsets is that they accentuate the flesh because they try to push it somewhere where it's not meant to be. Thus, the flesh becomes more important than the face – that's the beginning of 'roly-poly'. Mummy used a Yiddish phrase for it: *floysh mit oygen* – 'flesh with eyes'. There are synonyms for 'fat' – portly, stocky, curvaceous, busty, heavy – but roly-poly takes the biscuit.

RUDERY: This is a word I must have coined, because it doesn't appear in any dictionary online. I use it to cover the saltier strands of my vocabulary and story-telling, through which, thanks to *The Graham Norton Show*, I seem to have become popular. Potty-mouthed, dirty-minded, vulgar, even *vile*, are the adjectives I've inspired and I'm now refuting the justice of those epithets. There's more to me than filth; if all I said was centred below the waist, I would be a pathetic old thing, but I'm fighting back. Sex isn't dirty (if you clean your genitals, as I'm constantly urging), cussing is often appropriate in this changing world and my swear words are carefully chosen and no one has died as a result. You've stayed with me as far as the eighteenth letter of the alphabet and so I hope I've proved I'm also a thoughtful, occasionally even wise soul, always stressing the most essential words – 'kind' and 'compassionate' – when I can. 'Rudery' should not be the last word on Miriam Margolyes.

R

SANITARY TOWELS: Probably, I'm the only person alive now who has actually used sanitary towels. Tampax were invented in 1931 but nobody told Mummy, so in 1952, when my periods started, I embarked on my only piece of 'craftwork' – making a sanitary towel, under instruction from Mummy, with gauze and cotton wool. Menstruation wasn't popular. We called it being 'poorly' and it was literally a bloody nuisance. I don't miss them at all, I wasn't even very good with Tampax so when I had my womb out in 1974, we all heaved a sigh of relief.

SCORSESE, MARTIN: One director I had always longed to work with was Martin Scorsese. In 1993, my agent Susan told me he was casting *The Age of Innocence*, Edith Wharton's study of manners and morality in 1870s New York, and that there might be a good part for me. I was thrilled. The interview would be held at his house in Manhattan. I flew to New York and, one morning, took a cab to Mr Scorsese's brownstone house on the Upper East Side. I was nervous but excited. I rang the bell, a maid answered and ushered me into a library, filled not with books but with tapes and videos of films – thousands of them. Mr Scorsese came in and greeted me. He's a short man, with a kind smile and an intense gaze. He told me why he wanted to cast English actors in this film: the novel examines American society at a particular time when judgements were made about women, often cruelly. 'I'm interested in brutality, which can occur in the highest as well as in the lowest.' He wanted actors who could be authentically upper class, whose speech and bearing demanded respect and who carried themselves with confidence. He felt English actors were more at home depicting 'class' – we inherit it with our mother's milk.

My part, Mrs Manson Mingott, was an elderly lady of wealth and shrewdness, a loving grandmother, but a realist, keenly aware of the practicalities of life. (She is an upper-class version of the Nurse in *Romeo and Juliet*, who knows the ways of the world and respects its rules. She is the voice of Society.) 'I gave up arguing with young people fifty years ago,' she says placidly.

I had read the book and I saw in my mind's eye how I wanted Mrs Mingott to be. When I asked Mr Scorsese, 'Shall I be more serious?' he said, 'Absolutely not. I want her to bubble.' She was a woman after my own heart. Upon recovering from a stroke, Mrs Mingott, rather than retire into ladylike convalescence, organises a party. 'People were expecting a funeral,' she says, with a hoot of laughter. 'We must *entertain* them.'

SECRETS: I don't approve of secrets; they cause trouble. I don't have any secrets; I don't want any. And that makes me very strong. What you see is what you get.

SEMOLINA: Does anyone eat semolina now? I haven't seen it for years, but in the forties and fifties it was a regular at school dinners. We would queue up and the dinner ladies would ladle out the pudding. I LOVED chocolate semolina. It was definitely *goyische* food – no Jewish family would serve it. One dreadful day, I went up for four helpings. The first three slipped down deliciously; people marvelled as I gulped them. And then, I couldn't; I just couldn't spoon another skerrick into my mouth. I couldn't. The teacher on duty (I think it was Miss Brown, who had a truly astonishing hairdo: a Victory Roll on each ear) was normally a friendly soul, in charge of biology. She was conventional; a Christian who believed that greed should be punished. When I got up to leave the canteen, my pudding plate still full of my fourth helping, Miss Brown grimly advanced towards me. 'You will not leave this place until you have consumed what is on your plate.'

'B-b-b-but Miss Brown,' I stammered, 'I'll be sick.'

My plea fell on deaf ears. I remember the shame, hot tears pricking at my eyes as I stared queasily at the congealing pudding. I sat there until the end of the school day. Sadly, it didn't cure my greed but I've never touched semolina since.

SEX: Learning about sex for me was like learning to drive. I started with the basic vehicles while picking up the skills of gearbox control, and once I'd developed the proficiency, I had the confidence to take any car I fancied for a spin. The idea that a woman was supposed to feel pleasure had not been articulated to me and is a relatively recent concept. My **BIKE SHED** instructor at school, Carol Reay, was invaluable. My mother NEVER mentioned the word clitoris to me in my whole life. My first real experience of proper lesbian sex was in Leicester in 1966 from a skilled stage manager. Gosh, I'm grateful to her!

SHERRY: When I got into Cambridge in 1960, I knew fine well that a door was opening and it would lead to new and magnificent experiences. I didn't imagine one of the first dramatic epiphanies would cause me to vomit for three hours into a quaint Victorian lavatory bowl, blind drunk. At home, we never had alcohol around; Jews eat, they don't drink. I'd never heard of sherry parties, which were all the rage in Cambridge; it was how you entertained people in the Gentile world. So, in my first term I was extremely excited to be asked to a sherry party. The brand that everybody served was Tío Pepe, a dry amontillado. (Tío Pepe translates as 'Uncle Pete', which has a rather less sophisticated aura.)

So there I was, at my first Cambridge sherry party – a proper social gathering. The sherry was a clear, brown liquid, slightly viscous, served in a small glass. I swirled a mouthful and liked it. A lot. I refilled my glass immediately, gulping it down. I could hear myself talking and laughing even more loudly than usual. I felt I was hysterically funny, that my wit was flashing, positively ricocheting, round the room. Rather than slowing down, I speeded up and I knocked back glass after glass of Tío Pepe. In the end, I drank SEVENTEEN (I know, because I counted them).

Not long after that seventeenth sherry, I realised I was going to be violently sick. A kind friend guided me to a nearby lavatory. The bowl had a lovely Victorian design of leaves and flowers; possibly even an original Thomas Crapper. I knelt before it, raised the substantial wooden seat and spent the next two hours on my knees retching, staring down into the decorations, every so often spewing copiously. I couldn't get up; I was immersing myself in the new experience of complete intoxication. I gazed into the porcelain, absently admiring the pattern now imprinted on my memory for life. I gave up sherry there and then; once was enough. And I've never been drunk since that day.

SHIT HAPPENS: We were living in the cramped, North Oxford basement flat to which my parents escaped from the bombing of their Plaistow house in 1941. There was just Mummy and Daddy and me. I would have been about two, running around nappyless in the playpen, when Daddy's brother Jack and his wife Muriel came down from Glasgow to visit us. Muriel was elegant and slender, born in Dublin, a person who believed only in externals; not warm, but smiling as she bent down into the playpen. I had just done a poo and handed her, with a smile, my freshly minted present. She took it into her outstretched hand, suddenly realised what it was, threw it away and screamed and screamed and ran hysterically down the garden. Memory ceases after that, but we never liked each other and her loathing of me probably began then and simply increased as the years went by. Shit happens but blood is surely thicker than water. Not to Auntie Muriel!

SHOES: Because I have flat feet, I always wear trainers. Heather persuaded me to try Skechers; before that it had to be New Balance. I wear them every day, naturally to Buckingham Palace as well … I want to be comfortable. Sometimes I've had to wear smart shoes but now I don't bother – I just think, 'Well, tough titty, they'll take me as I am.'

SHORTS: I used to wear shorts to interviews. I like to be comfortable but the remarkable Susan Smith, my agent in America, gave me some firm advice. Obviously, it had been reported to her that I had appeared before some Hollywood worthies in inappropriate garb. She was on the phone to me in a trice. Usually, if I'd got a job, she phoned with the words: 'Good news for the Jews.' But this was different. 'Miriam,' she barked. 'DO NOT WEAR SHORTS TO AN INTERVIEW. EVER AGAIN, IS THAT CLEAR?' It was. (See also **HOLLYWOOD**.)

SHTETLS: The tragedy of modern European Jews is that the Holocaust erased not just the people but also every trace of our history. When I started genealogy, I had no thought of actually going to the *shtetl*s my family came from – those small villages where Jews lived and died, disliked and attacked for hundreds of years. When we made *Yentl* in Prague, the old Jews who had survived were brought to the set, to play the townsfolk. As they descended from the bus that had brought them, their eyes lit up with joy. A Jewish *shtetl* had survived, perfect in every detail. But when they walked round to see the backs of the little houses, they realised that was all there was – just a façade, cunningly recreated by the film crew. There was no *shtetl*. And their joy disappeared; they knew that way of life was gone for ever.

SMALL TALK: Money, sex, religion and politics are the things that we should be talking about. People shy away from these topics, frightened to cause arguments or heighten disagreements. But to me it's meat and drink, *exactly* the subjects we should make a beeline for. I'd be happy talking about nothing else.

SMITH, MAGGIE: When I was doing Harry Potter I got a call from my old school, asking for a bit of help. The current headmistress wanted Dame Maggie (another Old Girl) to come back to the school and open the new buildings; a carrot offered was that the theatre be named after her. Would I ask Dame Maggie as I was working with her? With some trepidation I agreed and broached the subject in her trailer at Leavesden Studios. 'Maggie, Oxford High School has asked me to find out if you'd come back and open the new buildings and a theatre space which they want to name after you.'

She glared. 'NO! No, I don't want to do that. I can't think of anything ghastlier. I loathed that school. It was so snobbish. I'm never going back there.'

Then she stared at me, beadily. 'Why don't YOU do it? You'd like that, wouldn't you? Tell them you'll do it instead.'

I reported Maggie's refusal back to the headmistress. After a slightly tense pause she said, 'Well, um ... Would *you* consider opening the studio, Miriam?'

I didn't waste a second. I didn't care about being the understudy. I went back to OHS, gave a talk to the whole school, was shown my name on the College entrance Honours Board and then taken to the little theatre space they had built. The plaque outside read: *The Miriam Margolyes Theatre Studio*. It was truly one of the proudest moments of my life. Maggie died in September 2024. The lights of the West End and on Broadway were dimmed. It's the highest tribute we actors can pay to the greatest of us.

SMOKED SALMON: I've always felt that smoked salmon was an essential ingredient of any social occasion. But it must, like a woman, be MOIST! And also, just like a woman, it must be responsibly sourced.

SOCIAL INTERCOURSE: I enjoy social intercourse. I don't pussyfoot and negotiate but there is an element of calculation involved. I don't think I'm ingratiating. I present that facet of myself which my instinct tells me is most acceptable. I am a many-faceted creature! I might praise where somebody else might not, but it's not just to make you like me. If you want to have genuine contact with people, they need a little bit of oil to open the door. But it has to be pure oil. You have to mean it. And I do.

SOUL: I just wish that I could be as perfect in my body as I am in my soul.

SPAM: Like everyone else, I am bombarded with obscene emails. The most recent I am sharing with you because at least it has a modicum of imaginative flair: 'Why don't you undress me with your teeth?' demanded Sharon John. (That'll be a first!)

SPEAK OUT: If I don't speak out against what I think is wrong, who am I? What can I say about anything? It takes away the point of being alive. Better jaw jaw than war war.*

SPICE GIRL: I was once asked what my name would be if I was a Spice Girl. I didn't have to think about it. 'FARTY SPICE'.

SPORTS SKILLS: I have never been sporty but at school I used my body as a weapon to great effect. My aim on the hockey pitch was to befuddle my opponents and make them laugh. I

---

* That's Churchill, of course.

was always lifting my Aertex shirt to flash my naked breasts and make them lose sight of the ball. And then WHAM! I knew that was my only chance to score as they doubled up with hysterical laughter. GOAL!! Once a Left Inner always a Left Inner.

STAGE FRIGHT: All actors suffer from stage fright because we're frightened to disappoint. Mine has only increased as I've got older. I'm not alone in this regard. Maggie Smith told me in Australia, when she was performing the Alan Bennett monologues in Sydney, that she often vomited before she went on stage. Even at the end of his career Sir Laurence Olivier had to be pushed onto the stage every night.

STICKY-BEAK: When I was younger, I worked for a respected market research company in London, called Norland. They trained me for two weeks and then sent me to my designated area: Henley-on-Thames. I had to approach people in the street. I was given a card on which were listed seven different methods of contraception and I'd give it to people and say, 'Now, which one do you use? Is it number one? Or number seven?' in order to spare their blushes, but strangely they'd always just say very directly, 'Oh, my husband withdraws.' Quite took me aback the first time. It was fun; it was a licence to ask questions. I was getting paid to be a sticky-beak. And I still am.

STYLE: My wardrobe is undistinguished, even absurd. A Scottish wardrobe mistress known for her dry humour, who was dressing me to play a tramp, once said: 'Oh, so that will be your own clothes, Miriam.' Cheek! I have worked up a certain style of my own, which I would call The Summer Frock – made of highly patterned, cotton material, the sort of dress young girls wore in the 1950s. These are often run up for me in the costume departments of various theatres and film studios in which I have worked. Not least as I demand side **POCKETS** and these are sadly now under threat of extinction, increasingly hard to track down in the concrete jungles of Oxford Street.

Shoes must be comfortable and dependable. I do impose orthotic insoles inside because my gait is uneven. Lord Byron, with whom I share a publisher, had a club foot, but I decided not to go that far.

My multicoloured socks are hand-knitted by my loving cousins Jenny and Katrina Cowan. I visit them annually to refresh the sock supply and to hear their intriguing stories of the Solomon family, one of whom, a former convict, sold old clothes from a barrow. Tramps run in the family after all.

SUPERSTITION: My mother was a slave to superstition. Shoes must never be left on the table. Ladders were avoided. If any sewing was done while wearing the garment being mended, a thread of the same cotton must be held between the teeth. Never look at the moon through glass. If you came out of the house and then had to go back in for some reason, you had to sit down and count to ten. If you praised a child's beauty you were required to spit through two fingers – 'p—p—p—' – to ward off the bad luck and say *unberufen* which is German for 'touch wood'. I'm not nearly so superstitious, but I never say 'Macbeth', quote from the Scottish play inside a theatre, or whistle in my dressing room.

SWEAR JAR, A WALKING: Now my Cameo fans always request foul language. CUNT and CUNT-FACE are favourites, closely followed by FUCKING HELL, IT'S A FUCKING NIGHTMARE. They seem to think that I'm some kind of swearing machine. Someone once described me as a 'walking swear jar'. And, of course, that isn't true. I use rough words quite thoughtfully. I know when I'm going to say 'cunt' and when I'm not. Swearing needs the impetus of rage rather than the lure of money to evoke its full colour. And it certainly destroys the *fun* – more than anything else in my life, I crave fun. And chopped liver.

SWEARING: The words we all use normally are quite, well, ordinary, uncharged. They're dulled by that banality. A swear word, on the other hand, still possesses a sort of dangerousness. Suddenly you're going to the heart of a very raw form of language. It pulses with a kind of electricity. It makes your skin prickle. Uttering a profanity can serve as a very handy escape valve for anger and frustration. I love swearing – I always have. Of course, it gets me into trouble. Mummy and Daddy hated it when I swore and I always had to apologise to them. 'It's not clever,' Mummy would say; 'I suppose you learned that at Cambridge.' I suppose I did.

SWITZERLAND: I'm not fond of Swiss things – except fondue. And Dignitas, of course.

T

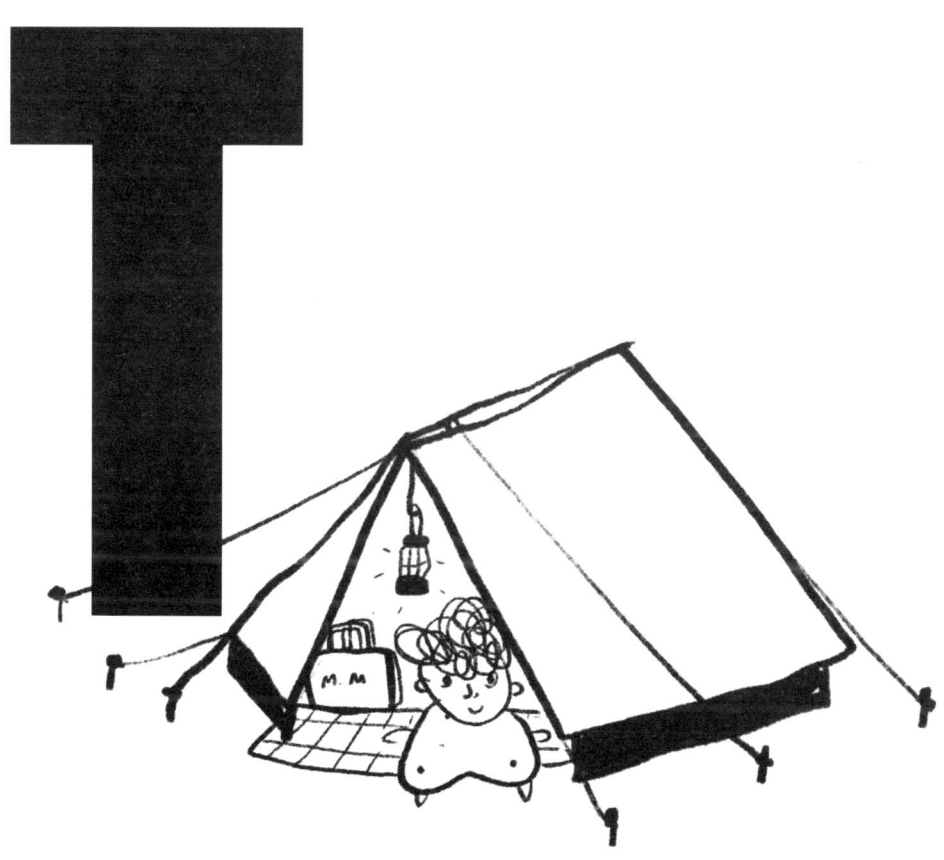

TALENTED TODDLERS: That's what my only therapist, Margaret Branch, used to call her show-business 'customers', of which she had many. After the initial interview, she said that I had an emotional age of about four; I was a 'princess baby splashing my yellow wellies in the puddles' and if I was exceptionally lucky, she'd help to get me to twelve. 'But that would be a triumph,' she added.

She often said, 'Miriam, don't be glib! Don't be glib! DON'T BE GLIB!' Important things were said three times; she insisted on focus. And always, after I'd handed her the 'brownies' (she insisted on cash paid in ten-pound notes) she'd sit in her chair opposite me and stare into my eyes. 'What about you, what about you, what about YOU?' she would enquire fiercely in a rising crescendo, and so the session would begin.

It was a long journey; we became extremely close. After roughly two years, Margaret said to me, 'I think I've done enough for you now, Miriam. You've reached your target age – twelve. I don't need to see you any more, unless you need a "top-up".' I visited her until she died; I cannot imagine a better therapist. Thank you, Margaret, from this talented toddler.

TALES OF THE UNEXPECTED was a popular Saturday night television series throughout the 1980s. It was the low-budget British version of *Alfred Hitchcock Presents*, adapted from the dark, short tales of Roald Dahl. These were sour stories for grown-ups – no chocolate factories or giant peaches here. Sometimes comic, always nasty, each tale told a sinister story of everyday folk, always with an unexpected twist in the tail.

I knew I'd been cast in 'Fat Chance' because I was fat, John Castle and Sheila Gish because they were damn good actors and pleasing to look at. But you always need to expect the unexpected. Tired of his obese wife and planning a new life with Sheila's character, Johnnie decides to bump me off with the one thing he is sure I can't resist. He buys me a box of chocolates he's injected with some lethal drug, and gives it to me, imagining I'll slowly poison myself as I gobble them up, sprawled in front of the TV, as usual. But he fatally underestimates me. He thinks he's the hero but, actually, *I* am. Here's a taste of the closing dialogue:

> **Johnnie:** So that box of chocolates I brought you was a waste of money?
> **Mary:** It was not a waste! I gave it to Frances.
> **Johnnie:** Frances? But she's gone.
> **Mary:** There was a strike at London Airport. Her flight's been delayed till this afternoon, so I gave her the chocs to take on the trip. I bet she's guzzling those soft centres now over the Atlantic and I don't feel a trace of envy. Not a trace. Now I'll make you a wonderful supper. We'll have grated carrot and lettuce and cottage cheese. I'll be as thin as a rake, Johnnie, and you'll love me. And you'll tell me you love me ...

TALK SHOWS: A talk show is an entertainment. It's *supposed* to be extemporised, to have the shine of unrehearsed artlessness. In fact, a lot of work is necessary to create that artifice. Most chat shows are carefully crafted and honed, but once your bottom is lowered onto the sofa and the audience ordered to clap by the studio manager, both guests and host are required to maintain the fiction of complete spontaneity.

But it's not a fiction to me: my joy comes in reacting to the moment. Something remarkable happens when you let go of what you thought you were going to say. Once we get involved in the conversation, anything can happen and I suck in the glories of the unrehearsed. The unexpected is insanely seductive. There's nothing better than a reckless conversation in which you are encouraging danger and skirting it at the same time. And luckily the hosts (particularly Graham Norton) agree – but not always the guests.

Once invited on a chat show, I say the first thing that pops into my head. The lovely truth is there are no lines to learn, no marks to hit. I can simply relax and that's when the naughty nuggets slip out, to discombobulate or dazzle.

From an early age I realised that dirty talk goes down well in most circumstances. But American talk shows were both decorous and tense. The guests can often be uptight on camera, preferring to hide rather than reveal. Back then even saying 'bowel movement' scared the shit out of American talk show hosts. Not me. I am determined to have fun, whatever happens.

T

TCHATCHKES is a Yiddish word for small gems and trinkets. My grandfather used to put his wares in a pack on his back and traipse around the lowlands of Scotland, selling tchatchkes to the miners' wives. He was a quiet, sweet man, liked by his customers who sensed his gentle integrity; they would save up and buy from him each time he came their way. Eventually, after many hard, precarious years plying his trade among the mining communities, he'd saved enough money to be able to buy a small premises in Glasgow in St Enoch's Square, and send his son (my father) to the best school in Glasgow, Hutcheson's Grammar. Daddy became 'Dux of Hutchie'. It's an honour, even if it doesn't sound like it.

TECHNOLOGY: I've become a LUDDITE again! I've got three computers, two iPads, three iPhones - and I'm not in control of any of them. I receive spam by the bucketful and it makes me worry I'll be hacked as so many of my friends have been. Technology, which has allowed me to do so much, has become threatening, scary and malevolent. I get that 'synching' feeling when YOU GOV, two-step verification and ONE TIME PASSWORDS suddenly shout at me. Zuckerberg, Musk (and other people I don't know) change my applications and interfere with my website and my communications. Unasked-for upgrades defeat and flummox me. Changing SIM cards is impossible and if I travel, I can't watch BBC programmes (always the best) without installing a VPN, something that makes me think of a Visible Panty Line – and that's a needless distraction.

I can't understand why my pet project – an initiative to help older people use computers I call 'Sponsor a Nanna' – doesn't inflame TV producers with joy. Without technology, the elderly are disenfranchised from everyday life. They can't use their bank accounts (and don't get me started about the impossibility of visiting an actual bank), use mobile phones, watch the channels they want, even get updates from their doctors. Why isn't there an army of young people mustering nationwide to help us oldies set up our technology and teach us to use it properly? Buck up Zuckerberg! Best foot forward, Bezos! It would be much more useful than spending billions gallivanting in space to give senior citizens a chance to engage. This isn't altruism. We could help with everything. We oldies have the money and the wisdom and the experience you need. It's no coincidence that the more we have been blocked out of the system, the more fucked the world has become. Don't forget that we faced down fascism before and won. Sponsor THIS Nanna!

TEENAGER: Perhaps the best thing about being a teenager is stopping being one, leaving behind the pimples and rages and anxieties besetting the years between thirteen and nineteen. But my teen years were so protected, so hemmed in by my parents' solicitude and my friends' warmth, that I felt little of the seismic physical and mental changes the youngsters today seem to experience. I left school still a child – and have remained so in many ways.

TENNIS: I've been told that I spend a huge amount of emotional energy on tennis. My parents met at a *Jewish* tennis club; I can't imagine the tennis was good, but the food would have been sublime. At school I played badly and quite enjoyed it but now tennis has become my passion. I've joined several tennis TV channels, I stay up all night to watch the matches if they're Grand Slams in another continent. I roar, scream, groan and generally make a nuisance of myself, which is why I don't actually go to the tournaments, because I would be ordered out immediately AND it's easier to go to the loo watching at home.

I do have a problem with the loathsome Serbian. I acknowledge his greatness as a tennis master but I abhor the tricks, lies, distractions and unsportsmanlike behaviour he exhibits on court. He's an arsehole – a gifted shit. However many titles he amasses in his greedy tennis bag, he can never touch the true GOATS – Nadal, Federer, Murray, Sampras, Edberg, even the jailbird Becker. And Graf, Venus and Serena, Martina and Billie Jean on the women's side. All GOATS, I refuse to pick one. Novak is the lowest of the low and thankfully, his tennis eminence is waning, but look out, world: he will bring the same deviousness to the political arena as soon as he can.

The good news is the ones to come: Alcaraz the glorious – honourable, loving the game, drop shots to die for, great shoulders; Sinner, the unlikely Italian – red-haired, polite, massively intelligent, lightning speed and precision; even our British Number One, Jack Draper. He should change the ridiculous baseball cap worn the wrong way round, but ooh, he's really good.

Watching tennis makes me happy and I bless Sue Barker, John McEnroe and the late Dan Maskell who brought it to me with flair and humour. Love All.

TENTACLES: Every acting job I have embarked on, each role I inhabit, has tentacles, which have reached out into my life, long after the performance itself has ended. Life is a kind of chain. You're introduced by somebody to somebody else and then to somebody else. And that's how friendships happen, how love affairs begin and end.

TENTS: I would have loved to go camping but my parents didn't approve; according to Mummy, 'Jewish girls don't sleep on the ground.'

TERESA, MOTHER: In 1993, the British Council invited me to tour my one-woman show, *Dickens' Women*. As chance (or God as she's otherwise known) would have it, we had arrived in Calcutta on the same day as Mother Teresa. I decided to seize the day and asked my driver if he would take me to her ashram in the morning. 'Oh yes, but you must get up in the morning. Very early.

Many people come. And you must take holy communion.'
I smiled and said nothing.

At 4 a.m. the next morning, he collected me and we drove to the ashram. A nun welcomed me and guided me to a huge hall, with many worshippers. After the service, we lined up to meet Mother Teresa; she was all in white, very small and brown, with an intense gaze. It was like a Papal Audience. When she looked at me, I felt she saw into my soul; a disquieting experience. 'How is it in England?' she asked me. I told her. Then, awkwardly, I handed her my offering, a large plastic bag of hotel toiletries I'd been collecting across my Indian tour. 'It's for the poor,' I explained lamely. She quickly handed it to an attendant nun. And our audience was at an end.

THATCHER, MARGARET: I couldn't stand Thatcher but she fascinates me. I always say she did more harm to England than Hitler; she certainly destroyed our Actors' Union (Equity), but she had a unity of vision, a remarkable commitment to her perception of the world and a determination to impose her will on the Cabinet, and then on the UK, which was unwavering. I hate her for what she did to the working class, selling off council houses, closing mines, but I would like to have met her and talked to her. She thought that Britain could be run like her father's grocer's shop. Well, it can't.

TODAY: I was thrilled when the BBC *Today* programme rang up and offered me a chance to celebrate my friend, Robbie Coltrane, who'd recently died.

I had returned from America the day before and was jet-lagged. On arrival a nice young researcher lady took me up to the waiting room. It was a shock to see Jeremy Hunt, a particularly Teflon-coated Tory minister, sitting there, surrounded by a small entourage like lagging around a boiler.

'Oh jeez,' I thought. I didn't know quite what to do, so I just said, 'You've got a hell of a job, best of luck.'

He smirked 'Thank you very much.'

I sat as far away from him as I could, and eventually he went into the studio. I was thinking about Robbie and what I was going to say. Then Jeremy Hunt came out and it was my turn.

As I got up at the end of the interview, I started to say, 'I never thought I'd be sitting in the seat …' Then it struck me that I might be still on air so I stopped, but Justin Webb laughed and said, '… that Jeremy Hunt has just sat in, is what you were about to say?' And when he said that, I thought, well, the mikes must be off.

'The thing is,' I went on, 'when I saw him there, I just said, "You've got a hell of a job. Best of luck." But what I really wanted to say was, "Fuck you, you bastard …"'

As I said the word 'fuck', Justin leapt up rather frantically saying, 'Oh, no, no, no, you mustn't say that. No, you can't say that! … We'll have to have you out of the studio now.'

'We will, with many apologies,' Martha Kearney added, continuing briskly. 'The time now is half-past eight, and time for the sports news …'

Overcome with horror, ushered by the young lady researcher, I tottered out. I said rather desperately, 'I thought the mikes were off. You've got to tell them that I thought the mikes were off.'

'No, it's all right. It doesn't matter,' she said, trying to calm me down.

'But it does matter,' I said. 'It's terrible!' I was imagining the listeners choking on their cornflakes.

In the taxi, I was still shaking, because it's an unforgivable blunder to utter such words on the nation's main morning programme – and I felt I'd let myself and Radio 4 down. I was still shaking when I got home. The whole thing was a reminder that sometimes you do need to button up. Robbie would have loved it.

TONE-DEAF: The sad thing is I look as if I can sing. I've got the breasts for singing; I've got the face for singing; I've got the pipes … for speaking, yes, but not for singing, alas. The tragedy is I took after Daddy, who was tone-deaf.

TOO FAT TO GO TO BED WITH: People have said, 'Oh, if you were skinny, Miriam, you wouldn't be the same.' And, no, I wouldn't be the same but perhaps I'd rather be a sharp, nasty but devastatingly sexy, skinny person.

In my late twenties, a lovely voice-over actress called Norma Mitchell said to me, 'Miriam, if you weren't fat, I would jump into bed with you in a minute.' I know she meant it in a nice way. 'Not much I can do about that,' I thought. But I've never forgotten the sting of it; in fact, I nearly called this book 'TOO FAT TO GO TO BED WITH'.

TORIES: Principles and compassion have disappeared from the Conservative manifesto. At one time the party was honourable; it had principles (even if I didn't agree with them) and included remarkable people. All that has evaporated. Blatant liars and incompetents like Boris Johnson and Liz Truss were voted to lead. That's who my mother used to call 'the best people'. She voted Tory all her life. Now they are truly the Nasty Party. 'Mummy knows best' (MKB) was her watchword. Maybe not quite ALWAYS, Mummy!

TRANS: I'm telling this story to honour the memory of a fine man and to show how words change their meaning as time goes by. I needed extra coaching in Latin if I was to get into university. Mummy found a perfect tutor, a Professor of Classics at Magdalen College. He was big and burly, smoked a pipe and wore country gentleman clothes, including a tweed jacket with leather-patched elbows. Every week I would go to his rooms in college for my lesson. He would stand in front of the fire, puffing on his pipe, and talk about the Greeks and Romans as if they lived around the corner. One day, some months after I had begun my tutorials, he said he wanted to tell me something. Naturally, I thought he was going to say that he'd fallen in love with me, because that's what you think when you're a seventeen-year-old girl. Instead, he said, 'I want to be a woman.' I was flabbergasted. He then said, 'May I go on?' Of course. He continued, 'Do you know what I'm wearing under my trousers?' He pulled up his trouser leg – and he was wearing stockings. I showed my surprise, and then he said, 'Have you noticed how smooth my skin is?' I said, 'Well, no, not really.' Though he did have a very good complexion. He took me to his bedroom, and showed me his dressing table. It was covered with emollients and perfumes and various unguents for the body, for the face, for the eyes, anti-wrinkle preparations, and every possible beauty formulation you could think of. 'Look at all my creams, that's why I have such smooth skin, because I use all these lotions.' I was astonished. Then he said, 'Have you noticed how small my feet are?' And he showed me his feet. I didn't quite know how I should respond to the sight of these perfectly normal-sized feet, so I said, 'Well, honestly, Tom, I've never really thought about it.' I was fascinated and rather surprised – very surprised, in fact. He replied, 'I want to be a woman. I've always wanted to be a woman since I was a little boy. I used to go into my mother's wardrobe and take out her dresses and wear them and look at myself in the mirror. I know that I'm meant to be a woman. I shouldn't be a man, it's all wrong.' He was practically crying. 'I have this pole, which makes me a man, and I don't want it. I want to cut it off. I don't want it. May I tell you the name I call myself?' Then he told me his true name was Agatha. It was hard not to laugh because Agatha isn't exactly the most glorious female name, but he said, 'May I write to you as Agatha, Miriam?' Naturally I said, 'Of course.' He wrote me letters signed Agatha and we were friends until he died. I still feel very proud that he shared his real self with me.

TRANS RIGHTS: As a person for whom grammar means honouring the structure of language (and a member of the now-defunct Apostrophe Society), at first I struggled to accept the importance of being 'they'. Then Zoe Terakes explained it to me: 'Why do you want to stop me from being "me"? Why is it so scary to acknowledge that gender is no longer merely binary?' And of course, I agree. What's the problem if 'he' becomes 'she' or 'they' – or anything else, for that matter?

When I was in Tasmania, I met Francine. Born male, after a stint in the military, she had worked as a teacher for nineteen years, and had married and had children. She told her wife and it was only at home, dressed in her wife's clothes, that she could become Francine. She had to wait till she was seventy-nine to have the sex-change operation. She wept as she told me her story: 'My life is now complete. I am who I was always meant to be.'

Anyone with a heart couldn't fail to be deeply moved by her story. Why should trans rights unnerve and infuriate to the point of violence those who describe themselves as 'M' or 'F'? Some people like chocolate digestives, others rich tea: I'm easy. Relax, for Christ's sake! Biscuits aside, I just want to make sure that there are enough loos for *everyone*. We're all human, aren't we – just not the same.

TRANSPARENCY is one of the key words of today, asking for decency to be visible, for legal and governmental process to be out in the open; for expenses to be admitted and secrets only to be TOP SECRET, not for everything to be shrouded and kept from public view. Politicians and the rich fear the light; darkness is their friend. But not ours!

TROJAN HORSE: When I was in school, we had been learning about the Greeks tricking the unsuspecting Trojans during the siege of Troy and this gave me the idea for my own wooden horse episode. Our school vaulting horse was constructed in a pyramid shape in a series of wooden tiers, which you could remove or add to in order to make it lower or higher, with the padded suede leather 'saddle' on the top for vaulting. My accomplices and I took the saddle off, I climbed in and the top was replaced, leaving me concealed and snug inside. By the time Miss Leonard, the gym teacher, came into the gym hall asking 'Where's Miriam?' my classmates were already in paroxysms. Through the grab holes in each of the wooden tiers, I had a perfect view of the unfolding scene. My chums could see my eyes darting about but Miss Leonard, somewhat lacking in energy and initiative, didn't notice a thing. I moved the horse just an inch or so. I could see that Miss Leonard was aware that it had moved, but decided to ignore it. Every so often, I would shuffle the horse forward a little more, inch by inch, watching her increasing befuddlement at every movement. She clearly hadn't the faintest idea what to do. It was exquisite fun. The entire class had collapsed onto the floor and were writhing in hysterical giggles. Eventually Miss L twigged and I got a detention but it was worth every minute of it – one of my best pranks.

TRUTHFULNESS: Truthfulness in friendship goes hand in hand with trust. You can't be friends with someone who lies to you. Truth is essential in friendship. You have to believe that you will each keep the confidences that you share with each other; that they're not going to talk about you behind your back, or betray and hurt you, and vice versa.

TRUST: 'Never trust anyone until hair grows in the palm of their hand,' my great-grandmother used to say. As we all know, hair never grows in the palm of your hand. It's a shocking lesson to teach a child, and sadly it is one that I have accepted. I trust everyone until they let me down, and then I never trust them again. But I don't close myself off from people and I never have.

Mummy and my father always felt that we were surrounded by enemies. I don't agree. I've accepted that there are enemies, but I've always known that my friends are my fortress, and for that I'm grateful.

TSURIS is a Yiddish phrase that means trouble, distress or aggravation. Everyone knows the 'Oy, oy, oy' wail of misery to which too often Jews have had to resort. Well, *tsuris* is the ill fortune which gives rise to such cries; it is not something to covet, cherish or desire. When I first went on holiday to Kingsgate in Kent, with my parents, I played with the non-Jewish little girl next door to our house in Percy Avenue. My mother overheard me asking her, 'Do you have *tsuris*?' 'No,' she replied, slightly puzzled. 'Oh, we have plenty,' I said, mirroring the adult cadence and confidently believing I had won that round.

TURNIPS: Lady Whiteadder from *Blackadder* of all my characters seems to have most resonated with middle-aged men. I don't know why, because she is a raving puritanical nutcase. Perhaps it's because she is so unknowingly bawdy, especially when she's getting her lips round that phallic turnip.

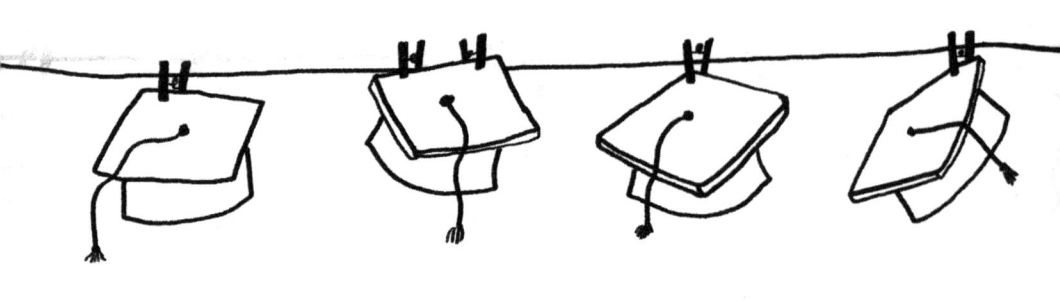

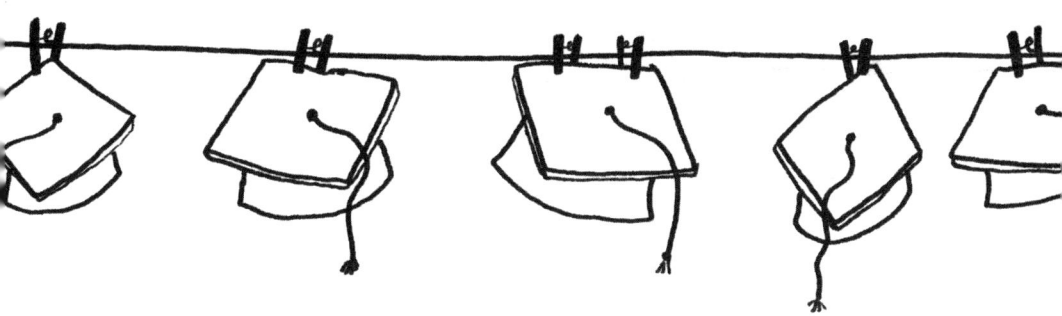

UMBRAGE is something that can be taken but not given, generally with pursed lips and folded arms. It suggests a peculiarly English offence-taking, one that feels mainly reserved for women. At least I've never heard of a man's taking it, but maybe they should.

UNCERTAINTY: These days we are all scared, both in a private sense but also because we feel the world we knew, or thought we knew, has changed immeasurably. Covid, lockdown, not seeing friends, no hugs allowed, left us secretly shaking with fright inside, uncertain of what we should be doing, saying and thinking; anxious about what our lives are going to be. And the lying politicians, especially Boris Johnson, left us ever more insecure. The sheer number of prime ministers revolving in and out of 10 Downing Street made us giddy and apprehensive. And we haven't recovered.

UNCONDITIONAL LOVE: I was extraordinarily lucky. The unconditional love my parents showered on me has protected me throughout my life. Even when I was not terribly successful

U at 'growing up', I knew who I was and, on the whole, I liked what I knew. They believed in me totally. And they told me so repeatedly. Did it make me conceited? Probably, yes. But it meant I could plough on through whatever disappointments lay in my path.

258 UNCOUPLING: I was on a train in Germany in the early sixties and noticed an attractive man sitting opposite me. The train slowed down: I looked hard at him, and he looked hard back. Then he got to his feet, looked at me again and I followed him out into the corridor and down to the loo in the next carriage. We locked the door and began (without words – my German is poor) a vigorous session. This did not include penetration but enthusiastic handjobs and, on my part, considerable mouth work. After he came, I suddenly realised what the metallic noise I could hear in the background was. In our *coupling*, we hadn't realised that the train was *uncoupling* itself from our carriage. In a flash, I was running back up the tracks after my departing luggage. Our encounter had been absorbing, but not worth abandoning my suitcase for! I managed to grab the last door of the last carriage and drag myself on. I still wonder what happened to

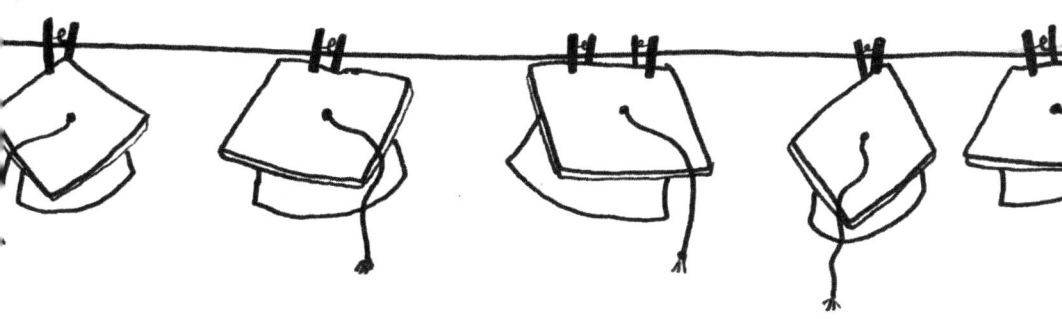

him, suitcaseless, left in the middle of nowhere with his trousers around his ankles.

U

UNDERGARMENTS: Mummy was fat and every morning I used to tie her corset strings tightly behind her back. Together, we fought the corset. I put my whole strength into tying the endless ribbons issuing from the bulky, whale-boned garment. I have never liked being trammelled in any way and the prospect of women's undergarments scared me. I knew I would NEVER cope with such a restrictive daily routine. I resisted having a bra for as long as possible but eventually Mummy and Grandma forced me to go to Elliston & Cavell where our neighbour, Miss Swinhoe, the brassiere fitter, corralled my nascent globes of glory into a flesh-coloured prison, which I hated. I did have 'roll-ons' as my tummy got

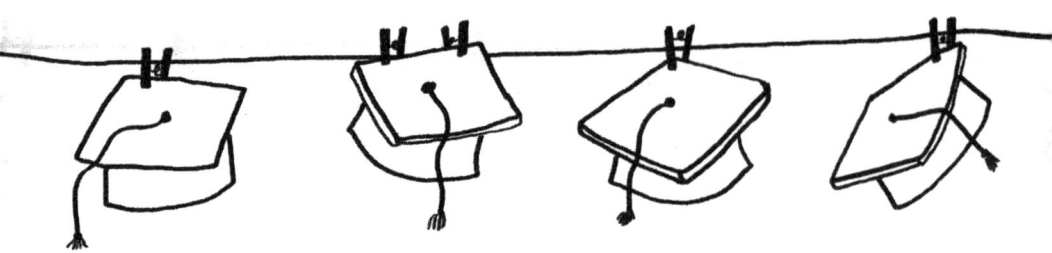

U

bigger, but now, as things have progressed, my tummy has become a belly and the globes of glory have obeyed the dictates of gravity and decidedly need support. (See **RAISING THE FALLEN**.)

UNDERSTUDY: I was only once an understudy – for Barbara Windsor. Standing in the wings just before the curtain went up, I heard that awful groan when the front-of-house manager announced that Barbara was indisposed and her understudy would be taking on the role. I had a brief second of utter horror and then thought, 'Fuck it. I've got to show them. They've paid! I've got to give them something.' And I did – I don't know how, but I did whatever I had to do for the two performances. On the following Monday, when Barbara came back, she came to my dressing room and said, 'I heard you was really good the other night, Miriam. I better watch myself with you. I'm not going off again and no mistake.' And she never did.

UNHAPPINESS: In my first year at Newnham when we would come down to breakfast every morning, there was a Third Year who was clearly desperately unhappy. There was an obvious aura

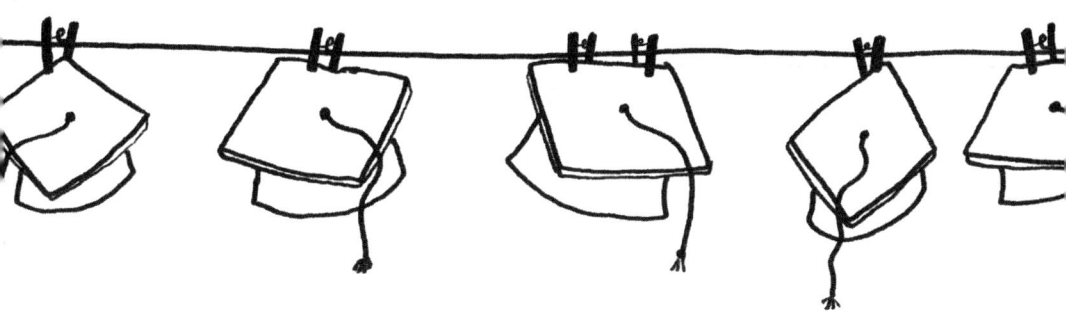

of misery and a despair about her. But she was a Third Year and we were First Years so we didn't speak to her. Then towards the end of term she gassed herself in her room. It was a lesson I have never forgotten. I decided in that moment I must never let an unhappiness go unremarked or uncomforted again, and if I saw anybody unhappy, I would talk to them – whether I knew them or not.

UNIONS: I strongly believe in unions. The weak and less powerful need protection against the ruling classes. Everyone should join whatever union they can.

UNIVERSITY CHALLENGE: In 1963, I represented Newnham College in the debut series of Granada TV's *University Challenge*. We travelled up to Manchester by train, a happy group. Liz, Jinty and Susan were all completely oblivious to the man masturbating opposite us. My masterstroke was to offer him a peppermint, whereupon he promptly detumesced. I should have kept one for myself. (See **FUCK** for the rest of the story.)

VAGINA COSTUME: My first appearance at the Edinburgh Festival was in *Ubu Roi* at the Traverse in 1963, directed by Gordon McDougall. I played Ma Ubu. The costumes were designed by Gerald Scarfe in the shape of the male and female genital organs. So I really was a cunt, and wore the costume! It caused a great fuss at City Hall – the usual uproar from staid Edinburgh aldermen trying to protect their citizens from filth.

VAGINA MONOLOGUES, THE: Forty years after I'd dressed as a vulva, I got to play one. *The Vagina Monologues* is a play by Eve Ensler where various women talk about their vaginas and various orgasms and, speech by speech and story by story, it all builds up to a huge overwhelming climax. I was in a production in 2001 with Siân Phillips and Sophie Dahl at the Arts Theatre. They both towered over me. Sophie was buxom at that time and truly beautiful, with creamy skin, long blonde hair and huge blue eyes. We had long honest conversations about our lives. Sophie talked wryly about her tough childhood, moving seventeen times by the time she was nineteen. 'All I wanted was a stable life but whenever I told Mum that, she used to say, "All right then, we'll get you a stable." It became a sort of family joke.' Every evening, Mick Jagger would pick her up at the stage door, looking like a debauched fifty-eight-year-old angel in tight jeans, his face perpetually grumpy. Clearly far from his only entanglement, Sophie was a former friend of his daughters Elizabeth and Jade, who were furious about the relationship. I'd never had much time for Mick Jagger but Sophie loved him so desperately that Siân and I worried about her. She may have been voicing a vagina in the production but if anything, he was the cunt. He was always so smug and a smug cunt is such a turn-off.

VAUGHAN, FRANKIE: Every time somebody came on television, Mummy would declare, 'He's Jewish.' We were thrilled when Frankie Vaughan got to number one in the hit parade. He was only called Vaughan because his grandmother said to him, in her thick Yiddish accent: 'Frankie you are my number vone [Vaughan] grandson.' I still look at every cast list at the end of television programmes to see who's Jewish. Frankie Vaughan's real name was Frank Abelson.

V

VICTORIA: I've always had a pash on Queen Victoria. For one thing, she was almost exactly my height (4ft 10ins) so even her clothes would have fitted me perfectly. But it is her character rather than her physique that inspires me. Her passions and wilfulness and enthusiasms are endearing. Her vivacity and intelligence leap off the pages of her letters and journals; her courage, good sense and sexual joy deserve wider appreciation. The Age to which she gave her name will forever fully engage my attention. I strongly urge you to read her diaries.

VISIONS: *Orpheus Descending* in 1988 was the second time I worked with Vanessa Redgrave. As before, her politics, shared endlessly with the cast, drove some of them crazy.
An indefatigable socialist and Trotskyite, Vanessa could and did bore the knickers off you talking about it. (And I say this as a believer, a former paid-up member of the Workers Revolutionary Party.)
   Vanessa was the incandescent star and I was the blind preacher's wife Vee who suffered from religious visions:

Vee: A world of light and shadow is what we live in, and – it's – confusing…
Val: Yeah, they – *do* get – *mixed*…
Vee: Well, and then – I heard this clap of thunder! Sky! – Split open! – And there in the split-open sky, I saw, I tell you, I *saw the* TWO HUGE BLAZING EYES OF JESUS CHRIST RISEN! – Not crucified but Risen! The blazing eyes of Christ Risen! And then a great – His hand! – *Invisible!* – I didn't *see* his hand! – But it *touched* me – *here!*
[*She seizes Val's hand and presses it to her great heaving bosom.*]

I fell for Vanessa more and more as the production went on. It was a schoolgirl crush – I was 'cracked' on her just like being back at Oxford High School. By the last night, I *had* to say something. I couldn't let the production end without letting her know. Just after the final curtain call, as we were all going off stage together, I blurted it out: 'You know I've fallen in love with you, Vanessa?'

She stopped dead, looked intently into my eyes and smiled sweetly and very tenderly at me. And then she said, 'But why did you wait till the last night to tell me?'

Vanessa's full acknowledgement of what I'd said turned what could have been a moment of mortification into almost a benediction. I loved her all the more for her immense kindness and tact.

VOGUE, BEING IN: Some ambitions are never going to be realised. An adult can cope with that. But some ambitions are never even considered to exist in the realms of possibility. I know what I look like, I know how profoundly disinterested I am in fashion, or rather, how profoundly disinterested fashion is in me. Or so I thought, but imagine my reaction when in January 2023, an email from Giles Hattersley of *Vogue* arrived at my agents.

> Well the long and the short of it is that Tim Walker is dying to photograph her and so I wondered if we might be able to tempt Miriam to sit for a series of portraits for a feature in *Vogue*'s July issue?
>
> Edward totally adores her. As do we all.

Of course, I couldn't quite believe it; especially that Edward Enninful, the then Editor of *British Vogue* even knew who I was. Flattered, I responded to the email with a YES PLEASE. And so it came to pass. On 18 April 2023, at 8 a.m. twenty people arrived and poured into the flat. It was not just the crew but such a vast selection of dresses, coats, shoes, bags, scarves, belts and fashion paraphernalia that all the furniture in most of my rooms had to be put into the garden so that the storage rails and chests of drawers could be accommodated. Luckily it didn't rain.

My stylist, Hazel, had chosen an amazing variety of garments, and there was a make-up lady and hair lady and a nail lady and an alterations lady and an especially kind person called Zoe, whom I've kept in my life since, because she is kind and knows where to get chairs mended. No one made me feel fat or ugly or incompetent. I said yes to everything, even when Tim Walker, the immensely distinguished photographer in charge, who seems ridiculously relaxed but oozes power and responsibility, suggested a nude shot. (See **ICED BUNS**.)

The shoot took all day, went up and down stairs and everyone knew what they were doing and were so friendly and funny that I forgot I scorned fashion, which I had until then; I completely changed my mind about the fashion industry and loved every amazing second.

At the end of the day, they brought all my furniture back in, packed everything up very neatly into their enormous pantechnicon and vanished into the night. The only evidence any of it had ever happened were my beautifully painted red nails and my new friends' numbers in my phone. And then I rather forgot about the whole thing. Until suddenly the July edition was there; it was a Gay Pride issue and I was – much to my delight and amazement – a *Vogue* cover girl. The phone rang off the hook. The edition sold out: Tim gave me the poster, which I treasure – it's on my living-room wall. Eat your heart out, Suzy Menkes. (That's a remark only Newnham Associates will understand!)

VOICE-OVER (See also **ADVERTS**): There is an art to commercial voice-over work. When you're creating with your voice alone, the focus has to be tight. I always ask the director to specify age and class. If you can centre your character accurately in a class category, it will be authentic. Then comes the geographical region. I always like to offer several readings to give them a choice. I believe I was easy to work with.

I enjoyed a joke and loved to shock. Sometimes, if annoyed with stupid directors, I'd pull up my jumper and frighten them with my bra. But when I was in the booth and working, my concentration was complete. The skill is in the timing, which was usually thirty seconds – the duration of most TV commercials. I was so famous for my accuracy that I could shave four seconds off if required.

My tips for doing voice-overs are not to speak directly into the mike and to breathe quietly (although with advertisements, the sound engineers can cut out the breath so that it doesn't get in the way). I always made friends with my sound engineers. They are as skilled as I am and their expertise can help me in so many ways. They can clip your take to make it fit the time, they can make you sound amazing. We are a team: the engineer and the voice.

By the middle of the eighties, I was doing about eight voice-overs a day, rushing up and down Soho, my pager affixed to my jumper and I was the top-earning female voice-over artist in the country.

VOLATILITY: People tend to think I'm funny and fluffy but I can switch on a sixpence from extreme happiness to utter despair. I'm aware that doesn't make it easy for people sometimes.

VULNERABILITY: It is the vulnerabilities in people, rather more than their strengths, which allow us to love them. I don't hide my vulnerability. I don't know how.

VULVA: The only people who explore your vulva are lovers and doctors; it's not a free-for-all amusement park. The techniques they employ are very different, mostly in the area of speed. Lovers tend to be slow and foreplay is important. But we don't want foreplay from our doctors – quite the reverse! Mr Studd, my aptly named first gynaecologist, was both matter-of-fact and friendly. He liked women and treated us with skill and humour. I never asked him about his attitude to clitorises (is that the correct plural?). But my word, he must have seen a few. The problem was, if I had a discharge, I didn't want him to see it, just to treat it. So, we talked more than he looked. But he always lubed with care and went in slowly. It's a habit I would recommend to all.

WARDROBE MISTRESSES: The problem for wardrobe mistresses is that I always need adjustment. They can't just put me into a dress and say, 'Perfect. That looks good, now off you go.' There's always a sigh, and then: 'Ah, yes, we'll just have to let that bit out a little and maybe put in a couple of darts.' In every role I ever played, I was *always* being darted. But in our business, you have to make your handicap into an advantage.

WEAPONS: In days of yore, when tits and hopes were high, I used to expose them – to charm, to excite, to diffuse anxiety and certainly to make people laugh. There are a few accounts in this *Little Book* of such harmless moments. But I can't do that now. The tits have ceased to be funny and an unexpected heaving (hoving?) into view would more likely cause horror than happiness. Guns are not an option, nor should they be. My chosen weapon is my voice. When accosted from behind, or menaced on Clapham Common, I simply take a big breath, open my mouth wide and ROAR! I was blessed with strong pipes and good projection; my virtue and vulva are so far unsullied. Grown men pale and flee when they hear the Voice.

    The other method is direct confrontation. A favourite recollection: when hastening along a BBC corridor, my jostling breasts caused lewd comments from the painters working there. On my return journey, I stopped, deliberately approached one of the miscreants and, removing his hands from his brush, placed both of them firmly on my breasts and held them there. He became desperate, struggling to release his unwilling digits from my globes of glory. Next time I passed them in that corridor – not a squeak.

WEIGHT: A battle I've never won, and at eighty-four, victory now is unlikely. Being fat is not yet a crime (as Daddy thought it should be) but it IS silly. My mother was fat but stylish. I never was, although now I have evolved a 'look' which I think is acceptable if not smart (see **STYLE**). But the belly – dearie, dearie me! That bundle of adipose tissue snuck up quite unexpectedly and is a devil to remove. I barely fitted into my coffin when I tried it for size at the Hastings Coffin Club meet; I might need an upgrade. The worst thing is when travelling. The humiliation of needing an 'extension seat belt' has to be faced. In order to deal with the shame, I call out loudly, 'I'm too fat for this seat,' and laugh, as if I weren't dying inside. Please: never be nasty to a fat person. They may sit on you!

WHATEVER: Once a bland unremarkable word, 'whatever' demands to be acted rather than said. Bordering on insulting, it has gone beyond the verbal and can be represented with both hands, thumbs touching, index fingers extending. Perfected by teenagers and appropriated by so-called adults, 'whatever' requires a curl of the lip and a contemptuous shrug of the shoulder. It is entirely modern, forged in the cauldron of the profound indifference which envelops us. Far ruder than any swear word, it is redolent of moral intellectual abdication. The only appropriate response is 'HOW DARE YOU!' followed by a resounding slap.

WHISKERS: However often you trim your facial hairs, they will outwit you and return. It does matter because HD (high definition) is all around us; the cruellest selfie can become front-page news; 'Jewish lesbian grows beard' is *not* what I want to see in the papers. I strongly reiterate my advice – never travel without tweezers and a magnifying mirror for the handbag. It's unnerving but essential to face the truth; whiskers, of all different sizes and thicknesses can grow overnight. Be ruthless; attack them, especially the tough, immensely long neck hair, that a kindly make-up artist thought was not attached to me until we both found it was!

WHITE LIES: The only time I allow myself to deviate from the strict truth is when I'm asked by someone who has just cooked me a meal whether I enjoyed it. Politeness insists that I say it was delicious, even if it wasn't; especially if they're Jewish. If I know the person well, then I allow myself to insult them, but it's really mean, when they've done their best, to say you didn't enjoy it. The difficult thing is that when my praise is too credible, second helpings are then proffered. The only thing worse is when the helping of something moreish, like chopped liver, is too *small*.

Oh, and of course, if the sex was not *quite* as delicious as one hoped, it's kinder to pretend. I've never given anyone marks out of ten, that's vulgar, but the great thing about cock-sucking (I speak from memory you understand) is that you don't have to say anything – indeed speech is almost impossible in those circumstances.

WHITE SNIFFS OF DOVER: An unexpected peril of seaside holiday rental is getting mixed up with a gang of drug smugglers but it happened to me. Two years ago, a Merseyside gang rented my clifftop property overlooking the Channel. I had bought the house for the view: they rented it for the flat roof. They needed a secret helicopter drop-off point for millions of pounds' worth of cocaine. The gang escaped to Thailand but the arms of the law are long and they were eventually arrested and banged up for twelve years. I wouldn't know if a gram of cocaine got up and bit me, so I was upset – but I admit it was also quite thrilling, like something out of a Bond movie. The trial was reported in the *Daily Mail*, unusually wittily under the headline 'The White Sniffs of Dover' and I was renamed Miriam Escobar.

'WICKED CHILD': Blokes still loom up and boom 'WICKED CHILD!' at me. Thankfully, they don't accompany it with Lady Whiteadder's double thwack.

> **Lady Whiteadder:** Chair! You have chairs in your house?
> **Blackadder:** Oh ... yes.
>   [*She slaps him twice*]
> **Lady Whiteadder:** Wicked child! Chairs are an invention of Satan! In our house Nathaniel sits on a spike.
> **Blackadder:** And yourself?
> **Lady Whiteadder:** I sit on Nathaniel. Two spikes would be an extravagance.

WILLIAMS, KENNETH: Kenny was the cleverest, funniest and saddest man I had ever met, fiercely opinionated about everything from why *Doctor Zhivago* was 'a pain in the arse as a film' to the agonising dullness of his fellow *Carry On* actors. Those hugely successful films that made him famous were packed with innuendo and smut. Yet when he told me he was celibate, I believed him. He pretended to be very shocked when I talked about sex. 'OOOooooh! Stooopp!' he would say with that famous snigger when it was plain that he was loving every salacious second.

WINGING IT: Being a show-off can have consequences. In the Third Form at Oxford High School, I was the form wag and therefore natural casting for Bottom, when we were required to perform a few scenes from *A Midsummer Night's Dream*. I thought I was so funny it seemed unnecessary actually to *learn* the lines of the play, I thought I could wing it. An expectant hush fell as we were about to do the famous scene when Titania awakes and falls in love with the weaver with the ass's head. And that's when I learned a valuable lesson: Shakespeare was a better writer, albeit four hundred years old, than I could ever be. Winging it can never be an option; since then, it never has been.

WOKE: Of course I am woke. And proudly so. 'Woke' is now used as a crude term of abuse for any liberal, left-leaning opinion – in the House of Commons, on the BBC, or scattered throughout the scurrilous comment pages of the *Daily Telegraph*. For the Tories, any opinion counter to their own is called 'woke'. I want to be woke. I wish everybody were. What they dismiss so cuttingly as 'political correctness run amok' is actually the kindness, awareness and tolerance essential in our increasingly callous world.

WOMEN ARE SUBLIME: I am still in touch with the bunch of girls I went to school with seventy years ago. Even when we haven't seen each other for a long time, immediately I hear those unmistakeable Oxford High School tones, it's as if we'd never been apart. We return to intimacy in a heartbeat. I think women are better at this than men. I blame the deep-seated male fear of emotion or any situation where tears might suddenly flow. Men clap each other on the back awkwardly, but women advance with arms wide open and hug and hug. Women are sublime.

WOMYN: I was once invited to a huge lesbian festival called the Michigan Womyn's Music Festival to perform *Gertrude Stein and a Companion*, with Pamela Rabe, a brilliant Australian/Canadian actress as Alice B. Toklas. It was August and very hot. I put on my velvet, long-sleeved, floor-length Gertrude Stein costume. I went out on stage; I took my pose in the Gertrude Stein chair and looked out to the audience. And that's when I became aware I was being watched by 4,000 nipples, give or take a few (not everyone had two breasts): sitting expectantly were over 2,000 enormous, and I mean ENORMOUS, lesbians, each and every one stark naked! (I don't know what it is about lesbians, but we're not known for svelteness. We're quite a chubby brigade.) There was A LOT of flesh on view ... I'm as big a feminist as anyone, but I should have been warned – and I am fascinated to see how Pam would cope. I couldn't look at her – there was a slight flickering of the eyelids; that was all: Pam is a Trooper. Now I always say, when you see 'women' spelt with a 'y', be prepared!

WORDS: When I am castigated for my 'potty mouth' I want to respond, 'Oh, so where do you stand on Gaza?' or 'Why has no one been prosecuted for Grenfell Tower?' And nowhere is this moral gap more clearly delineated than in language. However many times I say 'cunt-face' or 'shitbag' no one dies as a consequence, yet evil flourishes under the cover of bland terms like ethnic cleansing (in my book that's genocide) and Putin's 'special military operation' (also known as invasion). Truly scoundrel times!

WORKERS REVOLUTIONARY PARTY: If you were interested in politics in the late sixties, you wanted to stand up and be counted, and I was no different. I became a signed-up member of the Workers Revolutionary Party, inspired by Vanessa Redgrave, who was campaigning tirelessly outside every stage door in London then. Not long after I became a member, the WRP annual summer camp was held in an enclosed field by the Blackwater estuary in Essex; naturally I went along. Gerry Healy, the leader of the WRP, was an unpleasant, devious chap; he was dangerous in fact. There were talks and discussions in a big tent and Gerry would lecture us all about how to move England to the extreme left. Most of the other camp attendees clearly found it rousing: I found it threatening and nasty. I realised then that this wasn't my idea of a left-wing revolution, but the summer camp was in a beautiful place, and Vanessa and people like Frances de la Tour were there, so I stayed. In the morning, I thought I'd go for a walk with a chum. When we arrived at the fence enclosing the camp, a man with a gun was guarding the gate. He said, 'Where do you think you're going?' I said, 'For a walk.' He said, 'Oh, no. You can't leave.' I said, 'What do you mean we can't leave? We want to go for a walk.' 'Well, you can't. That's against the rules,' he said. 'No one can leave the camp.' And he put his hand firmly on his gun. We gulped. 'All right, love, keep your hair on,' I said and we went back to the Red House, our revolutionary hostel. Although I stayed to the end of that particular jamboree, that incident marked the end of *my* workers' revolution.

W

WRESTLING: Regrettably, I have to admit to liking violence. I don't want to encounter it personally but I love excitement, and crime stories and TV series delight me, and from an early age I enjoyed watching wrestling and boxing. Uncle Harold taught me about wrestling when I used to stay in Pollokshields in the 1960s. Under his tutelage, I learned to admire the powerful Boston Crab hold, the Headlock, the Camel Clutch. We watched the afternoon matches on TV and would shout at the screen and discuss the relative merits of Big Daddy and Mick McManus. I didn't know it was all a put-up job, I thought their screams were real, and I relished it. I still watch boxing and tennis and football, but I miss the roars of the wrestling ring and the vicious jumps and flattenings of these big, skilled men, gouging and punching and punishing their opponents.

WRINKLES: Many actresses despair when wrinkles first appear: I welcomed them. My wrinkles are the honourable traces of my life: laugh lines rather than frown lines.

X-RATED: It's all Marise Hepworth's fault. 'I'm doing some recordings for the Ann Summers sex shop. Would you like to do one?' she said. 'You get three hundred quid in cash. No repeat fees.'

I said, 'I don't deal in cash.' (I've followed my father's advice and have always been ferociously careful. All my income is declared, so I've never been in trouble with the Inland Revenue.) But at that time, £300 was a tempting amount. 'How do I get on to it?'

'Go to the Ann Summers shop, make an appointment, and the guy who runs it will sort you out with an audition.'

She reassured me that it was voice only – a take-home wanker's kit, basically. I had no problem with that. I went along to the shop on Tottenham Court Road. The chap at the till sent me to the cavernous warehouse space, at the back. There were no windows and the shelves were piled high with sex toys: scrotum twisters, ticklers, handcuffs, nipple clamps and dildos. Quite a cornucopia if you like that sort of thing. The man said, 'Oh, yes. Miriam Margolyes. Well, Miriam, I've written the script. Here it is, and the microphone is over there.'

I squeaked, 'You want me to do it *here*? In the warehouse?'

'I just need to know that you can handle it. We'll do the real thing in the studio.'

I started to read out his appalling script, which was full of heavy breathing, squeals, vocal intercourse and more. I realise for all my dirty talk, I'm prudish, and I found it rather unpleasant having to pretend to achieve orgasm in front of this creepy bloke. However, it was a job, I gave it my all, and my moans echoed back convincingly from the dungeon walls.

'Yeah, that was good,' the warehouse fellow said. 'When are you free?' We arranged a date, I turned up at the appointed hour and to my surprise I knew the engineer, David Hodge. He seemed a bit taken aback to find that I was the voice on this job, so I was all brisk and businesslike: 'Yes, I'm not sure how we're going to do it, but I'll just do the best I can.'

The script had no redeeming features and hardly any story. A schoolgirl called Sonia meets a man and then engages in several prolonged fucking sessions. Not many words, but so much panting and gasping and squelching. Simulating orgasms (and there were a lot of orgasms) involves a significant amount of heavy breathing and I had a bad headache by the end. Truly, one climax is much like another, but I was having to delve into my subconscious to achieve the variety I felt was expected. And at least if you have real sex, you have some fulfilment at the end – my only fulfilment was the three hundred quid.

When *Sexy Sonia: Leaves from My Schoolgirl Diary* was all finished and on sale, I wanted to find out how it was doing. I went into Ann Summers (full of browsing men all deliberately avoiding eye contact) and said loudly to the chap behind the counter, 'Oh, hello, I wonder if you could help me. I'm "Sexy Sonia" and I wondered how I was selling.'

The salesman froze. 'Shhhhh!' he whispered. He didn't want the customers to connect me with the tape; I assume he thought that if the punters saw me, they probably wouldn't buy it.

I said more quietly, 'Oh, sorry, I just want to know ... how is my tape doing? Is it selling?'

I was delighted to discover that *Sexy Sonia: Leaves from My Schoolgirl Diary* was a nice little earner. Not that it made any difference to me financially, because I didn't get any royalties or repeat fees, but it was a matter of pride to know that my voice was stimulating ejaculation all over the United

Kingdom. I don't have a copy now; do let me know if you find one.

XENOPHOBIA: Definition: a hatred of strangers. How very suburban, but we're all guilty of it. It's too easy to like only what we know.

YES: My last name is a bloody nuisance – always misspelled, sometimes as MARGOYLES, or GARGOYLE – even GARMOLYES. But that last one came from a drunken partner of my father's, who tottered back from a liquid evening and greeted my mother with an incoherent mumble, 'Good evening Mrs Garmolyes!' Once, on a BT phone bill, I was NINAM NARGOLYES – that took the biscuit. But the way I get people to remember is to remind them of the final three letters – YES, the most positive and affirmative final syllable imaginable. Latin knew how to do it. *Nonne* expected a YES reply, *Num* expected a NO. It makes life much easier.

YID, GAY: In 1965, I joined a group called the Gay Yids and proudly wore my Gay Yids badge when I went to the BBC. People, especially Patricia Routledge, found it rather shocking. I gloried in it, because I thought that being gay made me more interesting. I held Gay Yid parties at the flat and it was during one of them that Saul Radomsky, the great South African theatre designer, met and fell in love with the Israeli chef, Oded Schwartz. They stayed together till Oded died. Thus, I became a matchmaker for real.

YONI: Whenever I mention the word 'yoni' there are blank looks, particularly from blokes. Actually, I'd never heard it before I came to Australia to film in Byron Bay. There, yoni (aka jacksy) was all the rage. I joined a group of women, all dressed in long, loose dresses. There was a circle of chairs without seats. We sat on the chairs and spread our skirts over them. Then bowls of boiling water filled with herbs were placed underneath each chair. I requested garlic and oregano but everybody said no. I must have got it muddled with pasta...

I had lavender and mint and sage instead. And then you sit over this fragrant steaming saucepan and you park your labia and your legs and the cloud wafts up and just soothes the yoni. It's absolutely delightful. *Do* try this at home.

YOURSELF, BE: I was trying to think what's been the watchword of my life. And it is connection, wanting to be with people and seeing them absorb my personality and then my absorbing their personalities. But I've noticed that the conversation is wary now. People are too anxious about how they come across to the general public. And I have no time for that. You can't constantly be self-editing, because then the directness, the immediacy of communication I love, disappears. Be Yourself.

YOUTH IS WASTED ON THE YOUNG: When I was a teenager I didn't bother about my looks, certainly not the way kids do now. I liked my face, I never looked at my body – and if I could advise the young today, I would say: Try not to worry about what you look like. You're YOUNG! You lucky fuckers. Enjoy it! Just keep clean, keep reading, carry condoms and travel while you can.

YUMBO: My social media shorthand is somewhat limited. On Facebook, my only platform, when friends send me close-ups of their latest culinary excitement, as I can neither smell nor taste the offering, I simply write YUMBO! I hope this satisfies their need for approval.

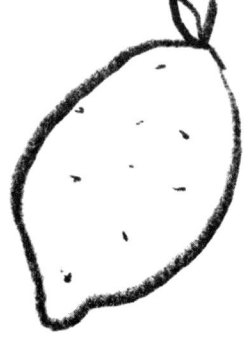

ZAFTIG is a Yiddish word applied usually to a well-rounded lady, who might promise more juicy joys. I love being called zaftig – it's a lot better than roly-poly.

ZEST: Acting is like a lemon, at once bitter and also refreshing. I can't do without its intensity. My identity is wrapped up in my profession. If I stop working, who the hell am I? How do I describe myself? Just a fat little old lady? You can tell yourself you're an actress all you like, but if nobody asks you to act, then what are you? Rejection becomes the norm. Is it sheer stubbornness to risk more doors slamming in your face or a sign of inner confidence? I am often asked where I find my zest for life; how have I kept going. Honestly, I don't know – it's just who I am.

ZIONISM is a political movement which began in Eastern Europe in the nineteenth century, with the object of creating a Jewish state in the Middle East. In the Second World War the Nazis tried to annihilate the entire Jewish population and nearly succeeded. Those who survived felt they had a God-given right to reclaim Palestine. Israel was finally established in 1948 but the fighting goes on. The big problem is Zionists refuse to accept that Palestinians have an equal claim to the land. That's where, as a people, we Jews failed, and where Hitler won. He changed us from being a compassionate nation into a destructive, uncaring and inhumane one. It makes me very sad. Everyone's afraid of each other – Jews are afraid of Palestinians, Palestinians are afraid of Jews. Everywhere I see fear, not understanding. Reason went out of the window a long time ago. The tragedy of the Palestinians is just as much the tragedy of the Jews.

ZODIAC SIGNS (PAH!): I hope I'm not a threatening lesbian. They do exist – I knew one once. She was an antique dealer and had apparently been, at one time, Britain's most accomplished cat burglar, spending frequent periods at Her Majesty's Pleasure (but not I fear giving her any). She had a lithe body, a deep voice and a penetrating blue-eyed stare which held you uncomfortably transfixed, but sadly her chat-up line was: 'Let me guess your star sign.' If she thought that would be alluring to me, she was dead wrong. Two topics terminate my interest immediately – star signs and the telling of **DREAMS**.

ZOOM: I spend much of my time on Zoom, a powerful, ubiquitous communications programme which the pandemic made essential. Grandparents used it most at first; wherever their grandchildren were, they could eyeball them, chastise them and disconnect when it got too noisy. I don't have grandchildren (phew!); for me Zoom is a good business tool for new job and publicity interviews. Our computers stare at each other; we often forget to turn on the camera or the sound or both. 'Can you hear me?' we shout at each other, looking interestedly at the background, which could be a cheat or really the journalist's messy kitchen or study. I love it when an interrupting dog or toddler proves that it's real after all. But the best thing about being a Zoomist is my fortnightly link-up with my old Cambridge buddies across the world, white-haired, bespectacled and hearing-aided, but still sharp as tacks. Our late night conversations in front of the Newnham gas fires continue sixty years on.

ZZZ AND SO TO BED: I'm always busy despite my natural mode being sloth. At the end of the long day, going to bed is heaven; I put my phone (which is my radio as well), my glasses, pills, whatever book (or books) I'm reading and a box of hankies beside me. My bed is a *matrimoniale*, an enormous double with plenty of space for nocturnal paraphernalia. My happiest moments are with Heather, gazing at the ceiling and talking about anything and everything. Goodnight!

Z

LET THEM EAT CAKE

But I can't leave you like this, after we have come to be friends. Well, I certainly hope we're friends – you now know almost everything about me, bar my PIN number. (If I have to change it again, I'll settle for Alzheimer's!)

    The last time I was on *The Graham Norton Show*, I brought Graham my favourite cake – made by my wonderful **LODGER**, George Naylor. As you know I never cook or do housework but George (the domestic goddess of our multi-generational household) once said he found cooking calming and so I've considered it a kindness ever since to demand regular baking sessions. Graham was clearly delighted with my offering (which I'll have to repeat if I ever get asked onto the show again) so I have asked George for the recipe for you to try for yourselves.

GEORGE NAYLOR'S COFFEE AND WALNUT CAKE

Miram is very particular about how this cake is made and after many, MANY bakes I think I can bake it in my sleep.

INGREDIENTS

Cake
175 grams unsalted butter
175 grams dark brown sugar
175 grams self-raising flour
50 grams walnuts
3 eggs
1 tablespoon coffee essence (Miriam demands Camp coffee*)

Butter icing
150 grams icing sugar
110 grams butter
1 tablespoon coffee essence
Walnuts to decorate

Mix 175 grams of butter with 175 grams of dark brown sugar. Once the mixture is light and fluffy, add a tablespoon of coffee essence, then slowly mix in 3 eggs (good quality free range). Then chop up 50 grams of walnuts (broken into small chunks, so they don't sink

---

*Not true – I like illy coffee but he's the chef! MM

to the bottom) and fold into the mixture with 175 grams of self-raising flour.

Pour the mixture into a greased baking tin and pop into a pre-heated oven for 45 minutes at 175°C. Check regularly and be sure check it's baked all the way through with a knife before setting aside to cool.

While it's cooling, it's time to make the buttercream: mix together 150 grams of icing sugar and 110 grams of butter with a tablespoon of coffee essence (more Camp coffee!). You may want to experiment with the sugar to butter ratio here: Miriam prefers it more buttery. Once the cake is cooled, cover it thickly with buttercream and decorate it with more walnuts.

At the risk of coming over all Marie Antoinette, it's all about the cake – and I want you to have it. Seize the day – and seize that cake. It's a good metaphor for life because now you can have another slice. Enjoy!

ACKNOWLEDGEMENTS

I want to thank the wonderful team who have helped to make *The Little Book of Miriam* happen: Georgina Laycock, chief midwife, the pearl of editors at John Murray Press; Denise Wordsworth, my PA and bookkeeper, who has held my hand through everything for twenty-two years; Sara Marafini for another amazing cover; Rosie Yates for her spot-on illustrations; eagle-eyed Charlotte Robathan and Caro Westmore in Editorial, Diana Talyanina in Production and Nicky Barneby for her clever design. Then there are the people who spread the word and got it to you: Sarah Arratoon and Kate Baguley in Marketing (thank you for the VOTE MIRIAM van); Charlotte Hutchinson and Leni Lawrence in Publicity; Megan Schaffer, Kyla Dean, Jess Harvey and Natasha Weninger-Kong in Sales and all my friends at Hachette ANZ and Ireland. Not to mention: George Naylor and Emily Cook – my new family, who live upstairs; James Albrecht, my generous producer, Mel Brown and all the great Fane team; Robert Kirby, Olivia Homan and Lindy King from United Agents – clearly the best agents in the world; Chad Ralston, Shaz Golshani my computer guru, and Barnaby Edwards and Rohan Onraet, the team who continue to gild my audio recordings and give me a golden gullet every time.

And a hearty welcome back to YOU, my dear loyal reader. Thank you for helping me to make my little book such a giant endeavour. Times may be dark but don't give up. Somehow I've been allowed to survive for eighty-four years and I've had such fun. Remember: be open, be kind, be brave. Let's Carpe that Diem and Save Our Souls.

CREDITS

Text of AnuSol advertisement © Church and Dwight, Bum's The Word campaign for AnuSol. 'Martha' by Walter de la Mare, with permission of The Literary Trustees of Walter de la Mare and the Society of Authors as their representative. 'If Your Breasts' by Ivor Cutler, with kind permission of The Estate of Ivor Cutler. *Orpheus Descending* by Tennessee Williams. Copyright © 1955, 1958 by Tennessee Williams, renewed © 1983, 1986 by the University of the South. Used by permission of Georges Borchardt, Inc., on behalf of the University of the South. All rights reserved. HARRY POTTER, characters, names and related indicia are trademarks of and © Warner Bros. Entertainment Inc. Harry Potter Publishing Rights © JKR.

INDEX

academia, 9
accents, 9, 25, 37
acting, 9–10, 78, 113–14, 141, 215, 246
  armchair acting, 16–17
ADC Theatre, Cambridge, 45
Adler, Moshe, 213
adverts, 10, 37, 147–8, 192, 269–70
afterlife, 10
Age of Innocence, The (film), 45, 191, 227–8
aging, 10–11
agony aunts, 11
air raids, 11–12
amateur, 12
America *see* USA
Andrews, Susan, 113
animals, 13
Ann Summers (sex shop), 285–6
answering machines, 13–14
antisemitism, 15, 130, 164
AnuSol, 15
apartheid, 15–16
apostrophes, 16
Ardern, Jacinda, 165
arsehole, 18
art, 18
'As the actress said to the bishop', 18–19

Asquith, Herbert, 69
Assenheim, Naomi, 129
Atkins, Eileen, 216
Atkinson, Rowan, 27
audience, 19
Augustine, Carole, 147
Australia, 19–20, 132–3, 194, 209, 291

Babe (film), 13
bacon, 23
Baddeley, Hermione, 23
Bade, Patrick, 18
Bailey, David, 23
Baker, Tom, 154
balls, 24
Baxter, Stanley, 192
BBC (Beeb), 24–5, 214
'Be Yourself', 292
Beatles, The 167
Beatty, Warren, 218
belly, 25
Bening, Annette, 218
Biden, Joe, 193
bike sheds, 25–6
Blackadder (TV series), 26–7, 93, 111–12, 254, 278
Bleak House (Dickens), 27, 56
Blood Wedding (stage play), 197
bowels/bowel movements, 15, 29

Branch, Margaret, 10, 241
bras, 215–17, 259–60
breasts, 29, 38, 72, 166, 215–17, 259–60, 275
Brexit, 30
Bridges, John, 24
Broadbent, Jim, 26, 111
Broadmoor, 30–1
Brown, Miss (teacher), 228–9
Buckingham Palace, 171, 205
bullies, 31, 43
burning your boats, 31
Burton, Richard, 31–3, 205
Burton, Tim, 119
Buscemi, Steve, 142
buttocks, 33, 37–8

Cadbury's Caramel Bunny, 37
cake, 300–1
Callas, Maria, 205
callipygian, 37–8
Cambridge University, 138–9, 197, 229–30
Cameo (internet business), 38–9
Cameron, David, 30
Camilla, Queen consort of the United Kingdom, 39–40, 67, 131
carpe diem, 40, 52

Casson, Lewis, 82
'cast your bread on the waters and it will come back sandwiches', 40
Castle, John, 241–2
centimorgans, 41
charisma, 41
Charles III, King of the United Kingdom, 67, 130–1, 171
Chase, Miss (teacher), 179
cheesecake, 41
children, 41
China, 85, 187
Christianity, 42
Christmas, 42
civil partnership, 189–90
Clark, Katerina, 219
cock-sucking *see* fellatio
coffin, 43
Coltrane, Robbie, 248–9
comedy, 43
coming out, 177, 181, 218–19
confidante, 43
confidence, 44
confrontation, 275
Conservative Party, 165–6, 204, 250, 279
conversation, 44
Cook, Lesley, 42
corpsing, 44–5
corsets, 190, 222, 259
costume drama, 45–6
Covid-19 pandemic, 109, 257
Coward, Noël, 59
Cowen, Jenny and Catriona, 236
'cracked on someone', 46
crisps, 46
Crossroads (TV soap opera), 27–8
cunt, 47
'cunt-face', 47

curiosity, 47, 207–8, 234
Cutler, Ivor, 217

Dahl, Roald, 119, 241
Dahl, Sophie, 265
Daiches, Samuel, 213
Daily Mail, 278
Daltons Weekly, 10
Dames, 51–2
Darwin, Lucy, 217
David (Michelangelo), 38
de la Tour, Frances, 281
death, 52, 57, 92
dementia, 110
Dench, Judi, 44, 51
dentists, 53, 89
Desert Island Discs (radio programme), 122
diamond, 53–5
DiCaprio, Leonardo, 55
dick, 55; *see also* penis
Dickens, Charles, 12, 27, 56–7, 77, 101, 130, 173–4
Dickens' Women (stage show), 56–7, 60, 246
dieting, 58
Dietrich, Marlene, 58–9
direction, 59
directness, 59
discipline, 59
Djokovic, Novak, 245
Dr Who (TV series), 143, 154
doctors, 60
documentarian, 60
Dodd, Ken, 131
dogs, 61
Donovan, Terry, 82–3
Double Take (stage show), 80–81
Drabble, Margaret, 219–20
dreams, 62, 296
drug smuggling, 278
dyke, 62

Ed and His Dead Mother (film), 142
Edinburgh Fringe Festival, 65, 77, 265
Edward VII, King of the United Kingdom, 67
Edzard, Christine, 191
'Elephant, The' (Asquith), 69–70
Elephant Ethel, 68
elephants, 68–71
Elizabeth II, Queen of the United Kingdom, 38, 171, 205–6
coronation, 203–4
elocution, 71–2
embonpoint, 72
Emily (lodger), 142–3
emotion, 73
End of Days (film), 17–18
Enninful, Edward, 268
Ensler, Eve, 265
Enter Solly Gold (TV play), 131
Evans, Edith, 98
exercise, 73
eyes, 73–4

face, 77
Face to Face (TV series), 123
facial hair, 276–7
Fagin (character), 77
failure, 78
fame, 157
family trees, 78
fandom, 79
Farage, Nigel, 3, 30, 193
farts/farting, 17–18, 38, 61, 79–80, 140
fashion, 268–9
fat/fatness, 78, 80, 222, 249, 276
fellatio, 42, 80, 89, 92, 178
Fields, Gracie, 159

305

First World War (1914–18), 53
Flaming Bodies (stage play), 141
Fletcher, Mandie, 26
Footlights, Cambridge, 80–1
Forster, E. M., 138
fortresses, 81
Frannie's Turn (TV series), 78
Fraser, Sonia, 56
free speech, 82
friction, 82
friends/friendship, 25, 60, 81, 113, 121, 164, 253, 254
  boring friends, 28–9
frightener, 82–4
frocks, 84, 192, 236
'frummers', 84
Fry, Stephen, 27
funerals, 86, 138

gagging, 89
Galanis, Steve, 38
Gallimore, Patricia, 99–100
Gamp, Sairey (character), 56, 89
Gascoigne, Bamber, 85, 262
Gay Yids, 291
Gaza, 115, 129, 158
genealogy, 78, 90, 232
generosity, 152–3
George Naylor's Coffee and Walnut Cake (recipe), 300–1
Gertrude Stein and a Companion (stage play), 280
gerunds, 90
gin, 90–1
Ginsburg, Ruth Bader, 193
Girl Guides, 93
Gish, Sheila, 241–2
gluttony, 91
God, 91
good advice, 91

'good girls', 92
gossip, 92
Gove, Michael, 30
Graham Norton Show, The (TV show), 66, 143, 222
grandparents, 41, 53–5, 74, 84, 152, 221, 243
graves, 92
Great Expectations (Dickens), 56, 100–1
great-grandparents, 30, 41, 253
greed, 228–9
groin-twitch, 92
growing up, 93
groynes, 93
guests, 93

hairbrush, 97–8
Hall, Peter, 52
handbag, contents of, 98
handjobs, 65–6, 99–100
Harding, Major, 72
Hardy, Miss (teacher), 18
'Harmony House', 100
Harris, Kamala, 193
Harry Potter film series, 153, 157, 195–6, 208, 232–3
Hattersley, Giles, 268
Havisham, Miss (character), 56, 100–1
Hayes, Malcolm, 215
Healy, Gerry, 281
Henn, Tom, 138
Hepworth, Marise, 10, 285
heredity, 101–2
herpes, 102
Highgate Cemetery, 92
Hitler, Adolf, 115, 295
Hobbs, Carleton, 215
Hodge, David, 286
Hodgkin, Liz, 60, 85, 139, 262
holidays, 102–3
Hollywood, 10, 2314

Holocaust, 77, 123, 164, 232, 295
Holroyd, Michael, 219–20
home, 104
homosexuality, 90, 176–7, 139–40, 181, 204, 218–19
  see also lesbians/lesbianism
horseradish, 105
housework, 105
Hunt, Jeremy, 248

I Love You to Death (film), 174
ice cream, 109, 204
ice-breaking, 109
iced buns, 109–10
identity, 110
immigration, 157
Importance of Being Earnest, The (TV drama), 198–9
Importance of Being Miriam, The (stage show), 53
imposters, 110–11
impulse, 174–5
incontinence, 111
Infanta of Castile (character), 111–12
intelligence, 112
internet, 112
intimacy, 113
intimacy counsellor, 113
intuition, 113–14
IRL (in real life), 114
Israel, 15, 114–15, 129, 164, 186–7, 295
Italy, 163, 177–8, 204

Jackson, Glenda, 12
Jackson, Miss (teacher), 152
Jagger, Mick, 265
Jam and Jerusalem (TV series), 192
jam, 119

James and the Giant Peach (film), 119–20
Jane Eyre (Charlotte Brontë), 121
jealousy, 121
Jesus, 121
Jews/Judaism, 77, 84, 114–15, 122–3, 186–7, 213–14, 232, 254, 295
  'Jewdar', 123
  see also antisemitism
John, Augustus, 123–4
Johnson, Boris, 30, 124, 250, 257
Johnson, Stanley, 124
jokes, 124–6
Joseph II, Holy Roman Emperor, 123

kangaroos, 132–3
Kearney, Martha, 248
Kenton, June, 216
Keren-Black, Jonathan, 213
kibbutz, 114, 129
'kike', 130
kindness, 130
Kingsgate, Kent, 102, 254
kissing, 131
knickers, 131
knitwear, 132
koalas, 132–3
Kops, Bernard, 131

Ladies in Lavender (film), 51
lady, being a, 137
landlords, 137–8, 142–3
laugh/laughter, 138
Laurie, Hugh, 27
laziness, 138
League of Health and Beauty, 105
Leavis, Frank and Queenie, 138–9
Lee, Susan, 85, 262
left-wing, becoming, 139
Leigh, Vivien, 174
Leonard, Miss (teacher), 253
lesbians/lesbianism, 43, 62, 139–40, 167, 175–7, 218–19, 280–1
  see also homosexuality
Levy, Naomi, 214
lift etiquette, 140
'like' (expression), 140
limelight, 141
lines, 141
Little Dorrit (film), 191
Little Shop of Horrors (film), 53
lodgers, 142–3
London, 143–4
Long Day's Journey into Night (Eugene O'Neill), 45
'look at me', 144
loos, 205
Los Angeles, California, 102
love, 144, 176
  unconditional love, 257–8
Lumley, Joanna, 119–20
lying, 144

McCoy, Sylvester, 153
McDougall, Gordon, 265
McInnerny, Tim, 26
McKellen, Ian, 181
Maddron, Miss (teacher), 163, 166
'make the most of it!', 147
Mandela, Nelson, 16
Manikin Cigars, 147–8
manners, 148
Margolyes (name), 149, 291
Margolyes, Jack (MM's uncle), 231
Margolyes, Dr Joseph ('Daddy'), 11–12, 40, 42, 51, 53–5, 73–4, 81, 92, 101–2, 114, 152, 176, 218–19, 243, 254
Margolyes, Muriel (MM's aunt), 231
Margolyes, Philip ('Grandpa'), 53–5, 152, 243
Margolyes, Ruth ('Mummy'), 9, 11–12, 16, 40, 159–60, 73–4, 81, 90, 91, 92, 100, 101–2, 105, 110, 119, 137, 152, 159–60, 176, 218–19, 221, 236, 237, 250, 254
marmalade, 119, 149–50
marriage, 151–2
'Martha' (Walter de la Mare), 102
Martin Chuzzlewit (Dickens), 89
Martin, Steve, 53
masturbation, 179
maths, 152
meanness, 152–3
Meep, 153–4
memory, 153
men, 155
menstruation *see* periods
Metropolitan Museum, New York, 155–6
Michigan Womyn's Music Festival, 280
Midsummer Night's Dream, A (play), 279
migrants, 157
Miriam (name), 157
Mirren, Helen, 113
Mitchell, Norma, 249
moderation, 158
money, 158
Monkhouse, Bob, 131
Montisi, Italy, 163
Monty Python's Flying Circus (TV series), 80–1
moral compass, 158
Mother Teresa, 246–7
Muir, Jinty, 85, 262
'murder your darlings', 52

307

napolitana, la (nickname), 163
Nardulli's ice cream parlour, Clapham, 109, 204
naughtiness, 163, 172
Naylor, George, 142–3, 299
Netanyahu, Benjamin, 44, 158
Neuberger, Julia, 214
New Zealand, 164–5
Newnham College, Cambridge, 24, 81, 85, 175, 178, 261, 262
NHS, 165–6, 204
nipples, 166
Noonan, Chris, 13
Northern Ireland, 166
Norton, Graham, 3, 61, 66, 243, 299
'Norwegian Wood' (song), 167
nose-picking, 167
nudity, 109–10, 113, 168

Obama, Barack, 193
OBE, 171
'Oh Miriam!', 172
old age, 172–3
Oliver Twist (Dickens), 56–7, 77, 130, 173–4
Olivier, Laurence, 174, 235
one-off, 174–5
onions, 175
only children, 176
openness, 176–7, 181
opera, 177–8
oral fixations, 178
oral sex *see* fellatio
orgasm, 179
Orpheus Descending (film), 266–7
ostrich, 180
outrageousness, 181
outsider, 182
Oxford, 137

Oxford High School, 26, 46, 55, 139, 152, 191, 196, 232–3, 279, 280

Pacific Palisades, California, 185
Palestine, 15, 115, 164, 186–7, 193, 295
pandas, 187
parking, 187–9
partner, 189–90
Parton, Dolly, 61
patriarchy, 190
Paxman, Jeremy, 24
penis, 38, 55, 178, 190
period costumes, 190–1
periods, 27–8, 191–2, 227
perseverance, 62
PG Tips, 192
Phillips, Siân, 265
Picasso, Pablo, 156
Pickwick Papers, The (Dickens), 57
Plowman, Mary, 71–2
Plowright, Joan, 174
pockets, 192, 236
Poe, Edgar Allan, 209
politics, 193, 252
popular culture, 193–4
potatoes, 194
Potter, Harry *see Harry Potter* film series
pranks, 196, 252–3
prisons, 30–1, 196–7
probation, 196–7
prompts, 197
pronouns, 251
protest marches, 148–9
'prunes and prisms', 198–9
Putin, Vladimir, 44

Quantocks, 203
quarrels, 203
queer, 204

questionnaire, 206–7
questions, 207–8, 234
queuing, 204–5
Quidditch, 208
quolls, 209
'Quoth the Raven', 209

rabbis, 213–14
Rabe, Pamela, 280–1
Rabin, Batya, 213
Rabin, Chaim, 213
radio, 214–15
radishes, 215
Radomsky, Saul, 291
Rayner, Claire, 11
Rayner, Jay, 208
Real Marigold on Tour, The (TV documentary), 187
Reay, Carol, 26, 229
rebellion, 217
Redgrave, Vanessa, 266, 281
Reds (film), 218
Rees-Mogg, Jacob, 9, 30, 155
Reform UK Party, 157
regrets, 218–19
Reid, Beryl, 18
reincarnation, 221
Reissar, Jenia, 149
Reith, John, 1st Baron Reith, 24
relationships, 219–20
religion, 10, 23, 42, 84, 91, 121, 122–3
restraint, 220
retail violence, 221
retirement, 221
riders, 221–2
Rigby, Terence, 198
Rigby & Peller, 215–17
Robinson, Tony, 27
'roly-poly', 222
Romeo + Juliet (film), 55
Rose-Neil, Sidney, 58
Roth, Michael, 214

Routledge, Patricia, 291
rudery, 222–3

Sackur, Stephen, 24
sadomasochism, 97–8
Sagar, Leonard, 137–8
Sandringham House, 67
sanitary towels, 227
Saunders, Jennifer, 192
Scarfe, Gerald, 265
Schwartz, Oded, 291
Schwarzenegger, Arnold, 17–18
Scorsese, Martin, 45–6, 227–8
Scottish accent, 9
secrets, 228
Selick, Henry, 119–20
semolina, 228–9
sex, 179, 215, 223, 229, 258–9, 286
sex education, 25–6
sexual fetishes, 97–8
Sexy Sonia: Leaves from My Schoolgirl Diary (Ann Summers tape), 285–7
Shakespeare, William, 279
Sheldrick Wildlife Trust, 70
Shelley, Norman, 215
Sher, Antony, 16
sherry, 229–30
shit, 230–1
shoes, 231, 236
shorts, 231
Shrager, Rosemary, 187
shtetls, 232
sleep, 297
Sleep, Wayne, 85
small talk, 232
Smith, Maggie, 51–2, 232–3, 235
Smith, Susan, 177, 227, 231
smoked salmon, 233
social intercourse, 233–4
social media, 38–9, 292

Soleimanpour, Nassim, 180
soul, 234
South Africa, 15–16
spam, 234, 244
Spamalot (stage musical), 122
speaking out, 234
Spice Girls, 234
sports skills, 234–5
Stack, Miss (headmistress), 172
stage fright, 235
Stand Up, Virgin Soldiers (film), 68
Stein, Gertrude, 155–6, 280
'sticky-beak', 235
style, 235–6, 276
superstition, 236
Sutherland, Heather, 3–4, 19, 73, 86, 104, 114, 144, 176–7, 179, 189–90, 218–20
swearing 84–5, 203, 222–3, 237, 281
swimming, 85
Switzerland, 237
Sydney Opera House, 188

'talented toddlers', 241
Tales of the Unexpected (TV series), 241–2
talk shows, 242–3
Taylor, Elizabeth, 31–3, 205
tchatchkes, 243
technology, 244
teenagers, 245
tennis, 245–6
tents, 246
Terakes, Zoe, 251
Thatcher, Margaret, 247
therapy, 241
This Morning (TV show), 11, 109
Thorndike, Sybil, 82
Today (radio programme), 248–9

Toklas, Alice B., 156
Tolkien, J. R. R., 165
tone-deaf, 249
Tories *see* Conservative Party
Tosca (opera), 205
trans rights, 251–2
transgender, 250–2
transparency, 252
Trojan Horse, 252–3
Trump, Donald, 12, 44, 110, 158, 193
Truss, Liz, 250
trust, 253–4
truthfulness, 253
tsuris, 254
turnips, 27, 254
Tynan, Kenneth, 84, 262
Tyringham Hall, Newport Pagnell, 58

Ubu Roi (comedy show), 265
umbrage, 257
uncertainty, 257
uncoupling, 258–9
undergarments, 259–60
understudies, 260–1
unhappiness, 261
unions, 247, 261
University Challenge (TV quiz show), 84–5, 262
USA, 12, 78, 185

vagina costume, 265
Vagina Monologues, The (stage play), 265
Vaughan, Frankie, 266
Victoria, Queen of the United Kingdom, 266
Vilnius, Lithuania, 157
Vogue magazine, 98, 109, 143, 268–9
voice, 275
voice-overs, 10, 269–70

volatility, 270
vulnerability, 270
vulva, 271

Walker, Tim, 109–10, 268–9
Walkinshaw, Miss (chief Guide), 93
Walters, Julie, 141
wardrobe mistresses, 276
Wark, Kirsty, 77
Warner, Jack, 102
weapons, 275
Webb, Justin, 248
weight, 276
Weinberg, Jacob, 213
West, Mae, 92
West, Miss (teacher), 191–2
Westbury, Marjorie, 215
Wharton, Edith, 227
'whatever' (expression), 276

white lies, 277
White Rabbit Red Rabbit (theatrical performance), 180
Wicked (stage musical), 191
'wicked child', 278
Widowing of Mrs Holroyd, The (D. H. Lawrence), 16–17
Wilde, Oscar, 198
Willetts, Miss (teacher), 196
Williams, Kenneth, 279
Wilson, Snoo, 141
Windsor, Barbara, 260–1
'winging it', 279
Winslet, Kate, 113
woke, 279–80
women, 80, 155, 280; *see also* lesbians
womyn, 280–1
Wood, John, 29

Woolf, Virginia, 151
words, 281
Workers Revolutionary Party, 281–2
wrestling, 282
Wright, Norman, 24, 214
wrinkles, 282

x-rated, 285–7
xenophobia, 287

Yentl (film), 232
'yoni', 291–2
Young, Roddy, 213
youth, 292
YUMBO, 292

'zaftig', 295
zest, 295
Zionism, 15, 51, 129, 130, 193, 295
zodiac signs, 296
Zoom, 296